Homebuilt .45 ACP Carbine

by

Gary F. Hartman

Published by

Gary F. Hartman
Lebanon, Oregon

Homebuilt .45 ACP Carbine

Copyright © 2013

All rights reserved. No part of this book may be reproduced or transmitted in any form, or by any means (except for the inclusion of brief quotations in reviews) without the prior written permission of the author.

ISBN 978-0-9815399-4-2
Library of Congress
Control Number 2013909190

Printed in U.S.A. By Lightning Source Inc.

Foreword

When I originally wrote "Homebuilt Firearms" in 2010, I was in the process of building a 10 shot .22 rifle from scrap steel, detailing construction as I proceeded with the project. As I got to the job of aligning the firing pin properly for the correct impact point to fire the .22 cartridge, which has a rimfire primer, it became obvious that a center fired cartridge would be a far easier model to build.

A center fire cartridge has a very large primer area, huge compared to the tiny rimfire area on the .22 round. I realized it would be great to also do a higher caliber rifle, but using a pistol cartridge. I especially like the .45 ACP for this, an excellent pistol cartridge.

Years ago, Marlin made a "Camp Carbine" in calibers 9 mm. and .45 ACP, however those were discontinued. Probably many firearms enthusiasts today would love the opportunity and availability of a pistol caliber carbine like .45 ACP.

In keeping with the idea of furthering build-it-yourself projects, this book is intended to expand the original idea in "Homebuilt Firearms" to allow building a .45 ACP Rifle or Carbine yourself.

Using a Bar Magazine concept as was used in the .22 project is the intent, but with the much larger diameter of a .45 round, the Bar Magazine must be stronger to withstand the 21,000 p.s.i. (pounds per square inch) that occurs over the larger cross sectional area. This sounds like a gigantic pressure, but keep in mind several steels available can withstand perhaps 75,000 to 100,000 p.s.i. or greater tensile stress. Pretty incredible! Even the .22 cartridge could generate 25,000 p.s.i. But over a very small cross section, it was easier to handle.

In the case of this project, it would seem a good approach to not only find a ready made barrel, but also perhaps have the Bar Magazine fabricated by a gunsmith, this to accomplish a safe Bar Magazine with the larger strength required over the .22 design.

With that in mind, the .45 Carbine project is described.

DISCLAIMER
****

In any project like this, the builder is 100% responsible for his own construction and safety. It is wholly the builder's job to do any checks he deems necessary through a gunsmith or other qualified person.

Also all work doing such a project has dangers: cuts, metal fragments, grinding dust, possibility of hot metal material or welding starting a fire, dust or fragments getting in the eyes, breathing hazardous material, etc. Avoidance of all hazards are the builder's responsibility.

Gary F. Hartman
Lebanon, OR

Also by the Author

Kids' Book of Adventure Projects	2008
Homebuilt Firearms	2010
Homebuilt Clocks	2011

Table of Contents

Chapter

1. Background and Safety — 1
2. The Barrel and Initial Magazine Construction — 6
3. Operation, Detailed Magazine Construction — 17
4. The Receiver — 27
5. "T" Bar and Positioner — 39
6. Hammer and Firing Pin Assembly — 52
7. Hammer Release and Trigger — 65
8. Hardening Critical Parts — 75
9. Finishing the Receiver — 80
10. Fitting the Barrel — 96
11. Using the Springs — 109
12. Testing the Rifle Mechanism — 115
13. Building the Pistol Grip Stock — 123
14. Finishing Up — 127

Chapter 1

Background and Safety
Disclaimer

    The purpose of this book is to explain the methods of building a large caliber homemade weapon that uses pistol ammunition, in this case a .45 ACP Carbine. **The construction discussed is my own, for educational purposes. Any attempt by a builder to copy my work is his responsibility and his alone.**
    "Homebuilt Firearms", my 2010 book, described a 10 shot .22 rifle, which used a steel Bar Magazine-- like a linear version of a revolver cylinder. This Carbine is similar, though not ten shots due to the much larger .45 cartridge, in this case perhaps five shots.
    The mechanical construction is almost identical but with additional safety concerns due to the cartridge. The .45 ACP specifications show a 21,000 p.s.i. Maximum Chamber Pressure. The .22 cartridge actually had a higher pressure specification, however, with the smaller cross sectional area of that round, the Bar Magazine could be smaller and lighter to safely handle the pressure.
    For the .45 ACP, we have a large cross sectional area, which makes for a much greater stress-- thus the Bar Magazine must be more substantial than mild steel, a better grade will allow a

smaller thickness. In studying gun crafts, and barrel materials on the internet, it appears 4140 Steel is the one usually used for gun barrels. It is a tough steel with a yield strength of 80,000 p.s.i. or more. So it should be excellent for this purpose. The Bar Magazine serves as the chamber for the round, the actual powder explosion occurs within, and thus it must withstand the force to contain the cartridge as it fires... basically the equivalent of a revolver cylinder.

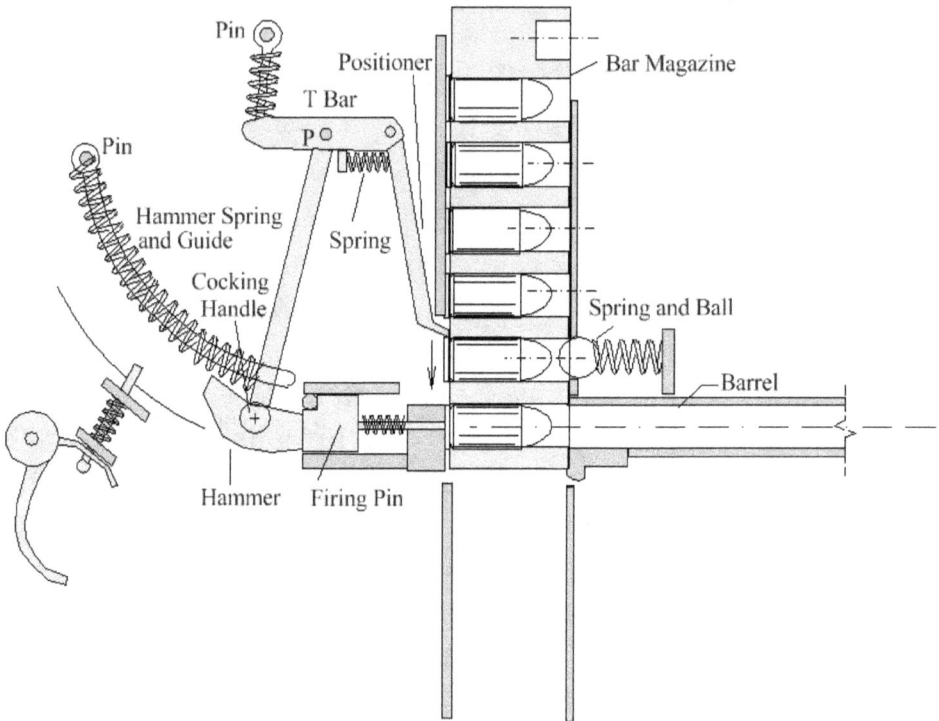

Fig. 1. Simplified Basic Mechanism

Before any work is done a barrel must be found. Once the barrel is obtained, the Bar Magazine can be designed. Basically the spacing of rounds is based on steel strength, the barrel size and the space available above for a steel ball and spring, which is used as a ball detent chamber lock for each position of the Bar Magazine. See Figure 1, a simplified view of the barrel and magazine.

Note in Figure 1 that the barrel assembly lies just below the spring loaded ball unit.

Once the center to center spacing is determined between the ball detent and the barrel... plus a space to allow fabricating the guide for the ball detent and some support for the barrel.... the Bar Magazine can be made.

General Description

In building the Carbine, the first portion was the Bar Magazine. That will be discussed in the next chapter. Then after the receiver and internal parts are made, the rifle should be assembled and tested several times at a distance, using a pull string for the trigger.

The final job is to build a suitable stock. Thus some woodworking is required beyond the metal work. In this final phase of the job, perhaps a Table Saw and other woodworking tools are required.

The stock will be a one-piece stock and handgrip. A forepiece or foregrip can also mount ahead of the receiver . The stock will probably be laminated with a plywood core.

Safety

In any project like this, there are several areas of work requiring extreme caution and adherence to safe practice.

- Metal cutting and drilling
- Grinding
- welding

Tools used will include a Bench Grinder, Angle Grinder with

cutting disk, Hacksaw, Files, Drill Press, also a Dremel type rotary tool with various cutting disks, and a Wire Welder. Before using any of these tools, you should familiarize yourself with the safety information of each, furthermore practice on some scraps before undertaking the real job.

Whenever you use the drill press always use the key in each of the three chuck holes to gradually tighten the chuck. This does a more balanced job with the sometimes crude chucks on typical inexpensive drill presses.

The thin cutting disks with the Dremel tool are extremely fragile, they essentially fly into fragments if bent while cutting. Be extremely cautious... ALWAYS wear Safety Goggles!

There are dangers from grinding fragments, chips, metal splinters, even fires during work due to hot particles flying off or blobs of hot metal from welding. Imagine if you shot some hot fragments into some fuel source in your garage... there is an endless bunch of bad possibilities, so before you start a process, think about the possibilities and guard against any sort of accident.

- **Wear a Full Face Shield preferably or Safety Goggles always**
- **NEVER change a bit or disk while a tool is plugged in.. ALWAYS unplug it first!!**
- **Avoid Flammables anywhere near your area**
- **Wear a Dust Mask if needed**
- **Wear Ear Protection for grinding or sawing**
- **Wear Leather Gloves for any hot work or welding.**
- **DO NOT wear loose sleeves which can snag or catch in spinning devices.**
- **Keep an appropriate Fire Extinguisher close in case of emergency**

- **Avoid touching hot metal from grinding, etc.**

If you just take you time for each process and think it through beforehand, you will glide through each process with minimal problems. Know your tools, and how to use them, practice if necessary to gain confidence.

Disclaimer for Construction

This book is written as a description of my building of the carbine, but is also written in instructional fashion. If a person should endeavor to copy my project, it shall be solely and entirely at his discretion, and his full responsibility.

In any case of building a firearm or any other project using dangerous tools and of course particularly a firearm which is dangerous in unskilled or careless hands, the entire project, workmanship, care and quality of the final device is entirely the builder's job, I cannot examine, approve or authorize any aspect of such a project not under my control. That job falls entirely on the builder.

Special Safety Note

I especially recommend a Full Face Shield over goggles. While I was grinding a piece on the bench grinder, a tiny debris fragment shot under my safety goggles, and stung my eye... luckily I was able to wash out my eye and nothing permanent occurred, however, a full face shield would have prevented this near miss. Our eyes are the most precious sense we have, take care of them!

Chapter 2

The Barrel and Initial Bar Magazine Construction

The first thing to do is locate a long .45 ACP barrel... unlike a used .22 barrel, it will likely not be a $10 item! In checking on the Internet and various gun part sources, the type and prices will vary greatly. It is possible if you have several local sources that you might locate a bargain, so do not omit checks amongst local shops, gun clubs, gun shows, etc. as you also look on the internet.

I found two types on the Internet... large diameter rough barrels that would require significant lathe work to reach a final barrel, and finished 16" .45 ACP barrels apparently made to fit 1911 type .45 pistols. A typical price would be close to $100, above or below. Here are three Internet sources:

- Green Mountain   gmriflebarrel.com
  $33 This is a 20" x 1" Diam. So it needs turning down to final diameter. 4140 Steel.

- Gunclips.net 16" finished barrel, approx. $90

- e-sarcoinc.com 16" finished barrel, approx. $90

The last two sources use a 16" barrel made by Roto 4M which is built to adapt into a 1911 Government .45 ... they have the rear locking lug, but none of this is of consequence for this purpose.

The first barrel is meant to be turned down to final finish, cost is low and it is 4140 steel, of excellent strength.

I used the Roto 4M barrel, but the following procedure would basically work for any barrel.

Prior to figuring the spacing between chambers in the Bar Magazine, some consideration of chamber pressure and stress in the metal magazine must be checked. The Bar Magazine will be made out of 4140 high strength Moly Steel, the same as used in most gun barrels.

I decided to try a bar 0.9" wide as a start and do some stress calculations. Look at Figure 2. which shows a cross section of a portion of the Bar Magazine with a chamber hole for the .45 ACP cartridge.

According to the specifications for 4140 Steel, it has a Yield Strength of 80,000 to 90000 p.s.i. This *Yield Strength* is defined as the maximum stress the 4140 Chrome-Moly can sustain without any failure and return to its previous state after the force is removed. It is a measure of capability of the material.

Figure 2 shows the cross sectional stress on the Bar Magazine due to the chamber pressure when the round fires. The pressure acts in a radial direction around the entire inner surface of the chamber. Note the small detail of a pressure vector... it can be broken into two components. One component is tensile and one is shear to match the situation in our bar.

There is a surface area of steel on each side of the chamber, which must contain the pressure force without the metal tearing at the centerline CL across the bar. The strength of this area of steel is the steel yield strength x Area of the metal on each side.

The area on each side is W x the Length of the cartridge case essentially.

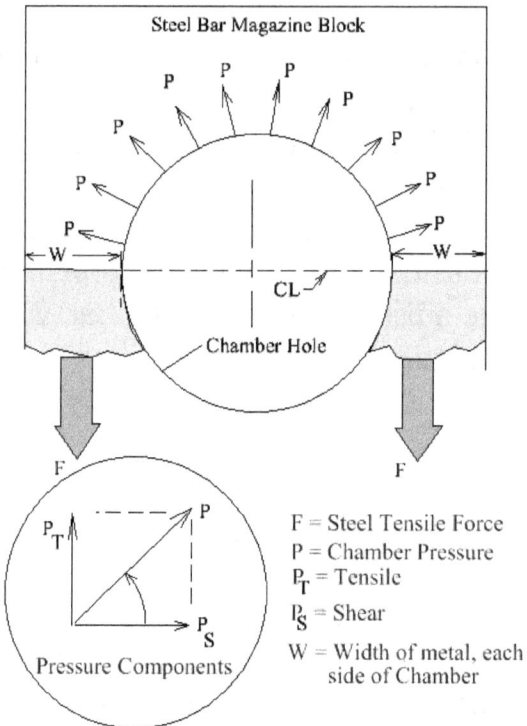

Fig. 2. Chamber Stress Diagram

The force trying to pull apart the metal is only the component pressure that is perpendicular the the centerline surface shown, the Tensile portion. The other portion, the Shear portion is essentially identical *along* the centerline CL. These are the two forces we must examine to determine safety of the Bar Magazine.

I initially imagined a bar approximately 0.9 inches thick. According to the specs by the S.A.A.M.I. (Sporting Arms and

Ammunition Manufacturers' Institute..)the chamber diameter for a .45 ACP is 0.4796". This dimension x the length of the cartridge case proper (0.698") gives the cross sectional area that the pressure acts upon in the chamber. The maximum pressure for a .45 ACP is listed as 21,000 p.s.i. So using this data, the force trying to blow the chamber apart at the instant of firing is approximately:

21,000 lb/sq in. x (0.480 x 0.698) Sq In. = 7036 lb force.

This force is essentially split between the two steel sides of the Bar Magazine... and basically equates to 3518 lb force per side.

Opposing this is the steel capability, *Tensile Force* which is the area of each side, Steel strength x (W x the casing length)...

Plugging in some values, assuming 80,000 p.s.i. For the steel:

80,000 lb/sq in. x ((0.9-.480) x 0.698) sq in. = 23450 lb capability.. the steel is quite safe with our round.

Any *Shear Force* trying to blow through the side is the same as the tensile equivalent situation and the thickness of metal is 0.210 thick, offering the same capability in Shear.

So this gives a nice factor of safety and using the 4140 Steel bar, 0.9" thick should easily handle the .45 ACP cartridge in the dimensions picked.

It would be possible to allow a gunsmith to recommend a smaller size bar to allow a lighter Bar Magazine, but the rest of this book and my construction will still use the Bar Magazine shown in Figure 3. Drilling those holes out will lighten the bar significantly.

Looking at Figure 3 shows the 4.30" bar height magazine as carrying five rounds, the top hole is only to index for the last shot, it should be drilled to a good depth just to cut weight but houses no cartridge.

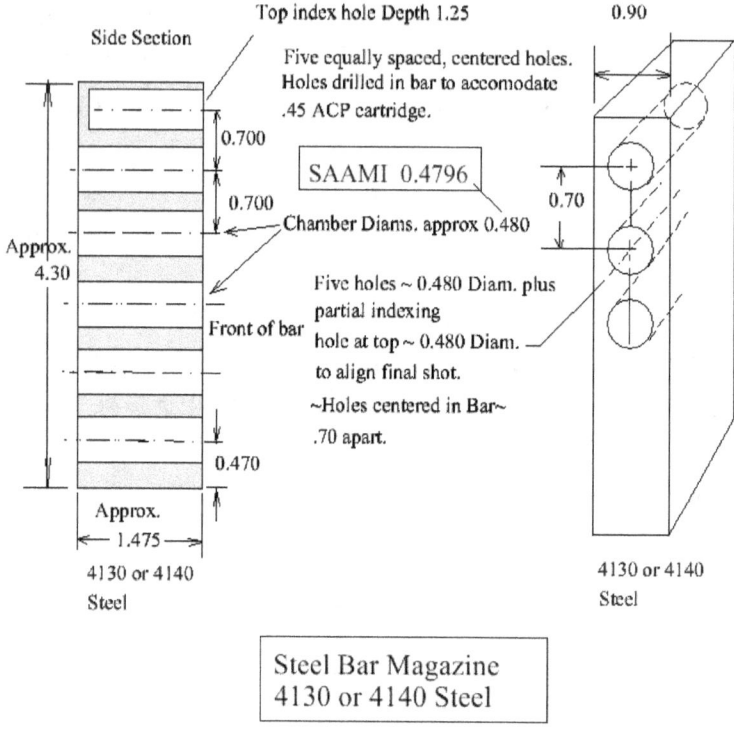

Fig. 3. Bar Magazine

    Because of the difficulty in accurately drilling this large a hole as well as the difficulty in accurately spacing the holes with usual garage tools, I recommend having some help, with the Bar Magazine piece drilled and reamed by a machinist.

    However, if you follow specific rules and setup in your construction, and have an X-Y cross slide assembly calibrated in thousandths for use with your drill press, you possibly could do a satisfactory job yourself if you have a large drill press.

    On many parts made for the rifle, there can be several ways to achieve a given result. You can cut a notch or step in a part, say for a limit or stop... or you can drill and set a pin to achieve the same result... either way is still a workable solution. So keep that in mind as the build proceeds.

Fig. 4. X-Y Cross Slide

If you wish to make your Bar Magazine yourself, keep these thoughts in mind:
- It would require very careful measurements and care in using the cross slide. Basically this device is a vise type assembly with calibrated .001 movement in both X and Y directions for precision drilling or milling. It clamps in a drill press work table to allow precision movement of the work piece during drilling, etc.

- Another thing to be aware of is the force that can deflect the drill table off level during drilling. Especially with large holes requiring significant drill pressure and a simple bench drill press… the drill impinging on the workpiece can deflect the worktable surface downward a bit at the outward unsupported edge lowering it compared to the clamped surface at the drill press support shaft. This means any hole through the piece is not perfectly perpendicular to the drilled surface.

- You would need to cut a suitable support block to fit snug beneath that unsupported edge before drilling. Then as you drill, it will support the edge to maintain a perpendicular hole alignment.

- One item I need to mention here is the size of your drill press.. If you have a small bench drill press, the X-Y Cross slide would mount onto the base, not the drill table, alleviating the support problem. See Figure 5. But this drill press is probably inadequate for drilling the Bar Magazine.

- After drilling, the holes should be reamed to just accept a .45 ACP cartridge.

You realize from this slight description that unless you have the specific equipment,
- The drill bit, 15/32"
- The reamer,
- The cross feed X-Y table, and
- A large drill press, a type which will accept the X-Y table---

and experience... you are better off to let a machinist help do this piece.

Hopefully an acquaintance or friend and gun enthusiast with mechanical abilities and a shop could help here. It will be nothing more than a block of steel with drilled and reamed holes at this point-- it is NOT a Bar Magazine yet. In my case I found

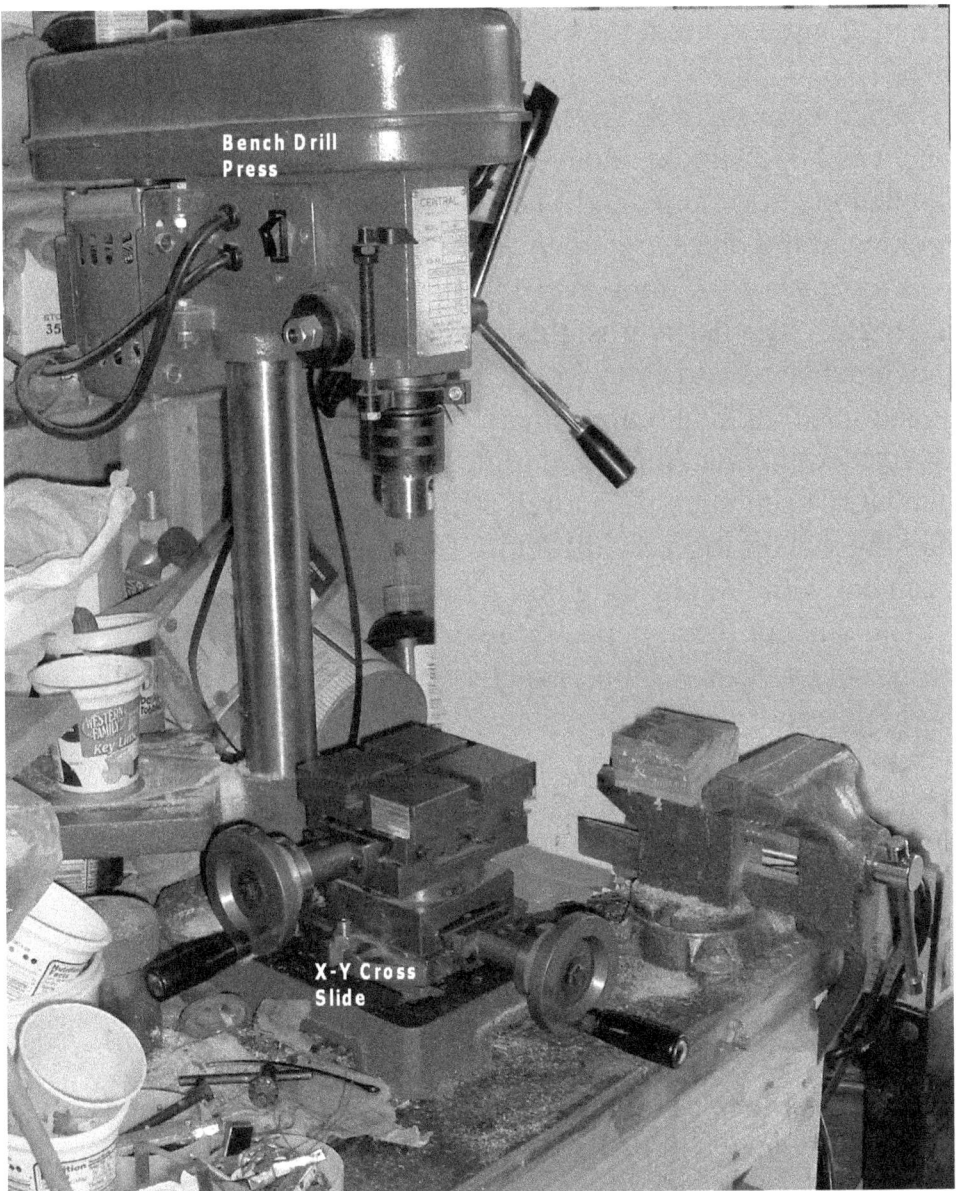

Fig. 5. Cross Slide on Drill Press

a machinist who would do it quite reasonably.

An odd thing occurred in seeking a piece of 4140 Steel for my magazine. I called around to find a small piece, hopefully a cutoff from some big shop job, and located a local firm, South Fork Industrial right here in Lebanon, OR. A gentleman named Brian assured me that they did have some small cutoffs of 4140 Steel.

When I got there to look, Brian showed me some scraps, and one was 1 1/2" thick... note the 1.475 dimension in Figure 3. he handed me the chunk, and I headed home. At home, I kept looking at the piece, and then measured the cross dimension... it was just over 4.35" and on top of that the remaining side was 8" in length! In other words, this chunk was absolutely perfect in the dimensions and even would allow several magazines to be sliced from it like a loaf of bread!

Further, the machinist had told me to be sure to get a piece that had NOT been cut with a torch as that would harden the surface making machining very difficult. Lo and behold, the piece had been cut with the old style liquid lubed power hacksaw.

Think about those items, three dimensions, and the cutting requirement, four for four, exactly correct. God wanted me to build this gun!

Looking at my situation, buying the barrel and having two Bar Magazines drilled and reamed by a machinist... the investment so far is a bit under $200.

These are the only critical parts, and the rest is essentially careful garage work with scrap sheet steel! Finally adding springs, and making a wooden stock.

Figure 6 shows the bored Bar Magazine; Figure 7 shows the barrel.

There is more detailed construction required for the Bar Magazine; that will be discussed in Chapter 3.

Special Note on the Drill Press Chuck

A note on the drill press chuck. Always use all three key jaw positions when tightening a bit into the chuck. This gives a more secure and even tightening process with the chucks typically installed on these bench drill presses.

Fig. 6. The Bar Magazine

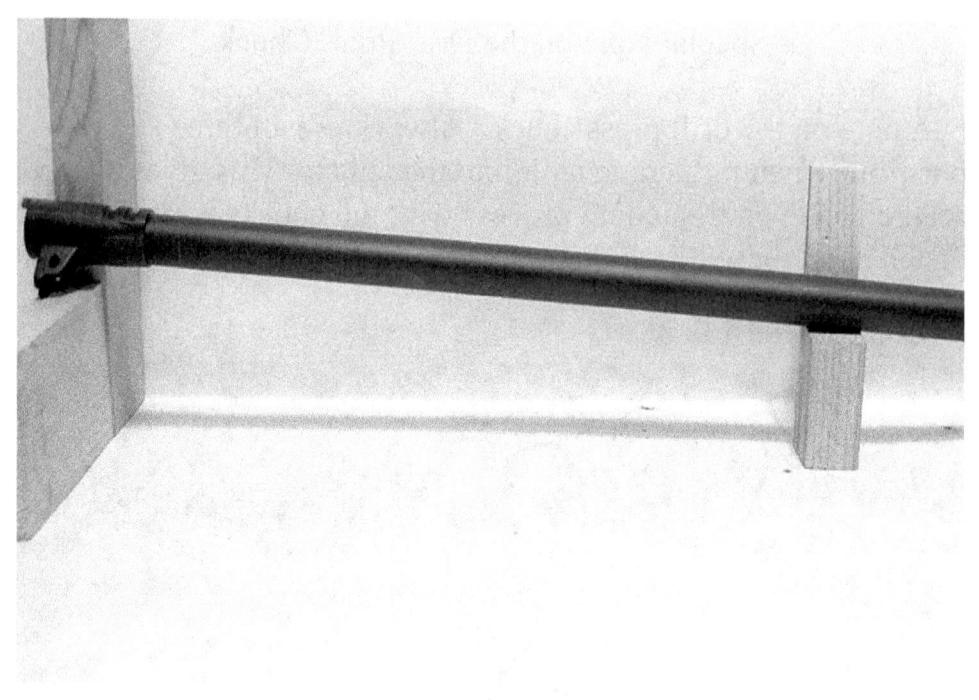

Fig. 7. Roto 4M Gun Barrel

Chapter 3

Description of Operation
and Detailed Bar Magazine Construction

In a nearby town is a Fabrication Shop with a scrap steel bin emptied every so often, as long as you hit it before the pickup day, you may buy pieces of scrap you salvage from the bin. For the rifle receiver an ideal pick is 12 and 14 gauge pieces, usually there are sheared pieces perfect for this purpose. Also something in 1/4" or 1/2" would be nice for making the heavier piece to form the breech at the rear of the chamber in the Bar Magazine area. This area would need to be strong and allow a nice firing pin channel to the rear of the cartridge.

Cutting the thin gauge steel is very easy with an Angle Grinder equipped with a cutoff disc. Even thicker pieces can be cut out rough for various parts, and a Bench Grinder and files can be used to fine tune and finish the small parts that go into the rifle.

Figure 8 on the next page shows the general look envisioned for the action, a repeater version of the carbine. Studying this diagram will illustrate the general operation of the rifle and show those items that are most critical. It is a very simple concept with minimal moving parts.

The parts are mostly made from scraps of 12 or 14 gauge steel, the Positioner spring is a small compression spring. The "T" Bar

is a unit; as it rotates during cocking, the Positioner moves downward, catching the cartridge rim and forcing the Bar Magazine to move down until the front hole of the Bar Magazine above the round is captured by the detent ball. This locks the round in alignment with the barrel simultaneously as the hammer locks at the release mechanism.
The conventional compression springs are from Amazon.

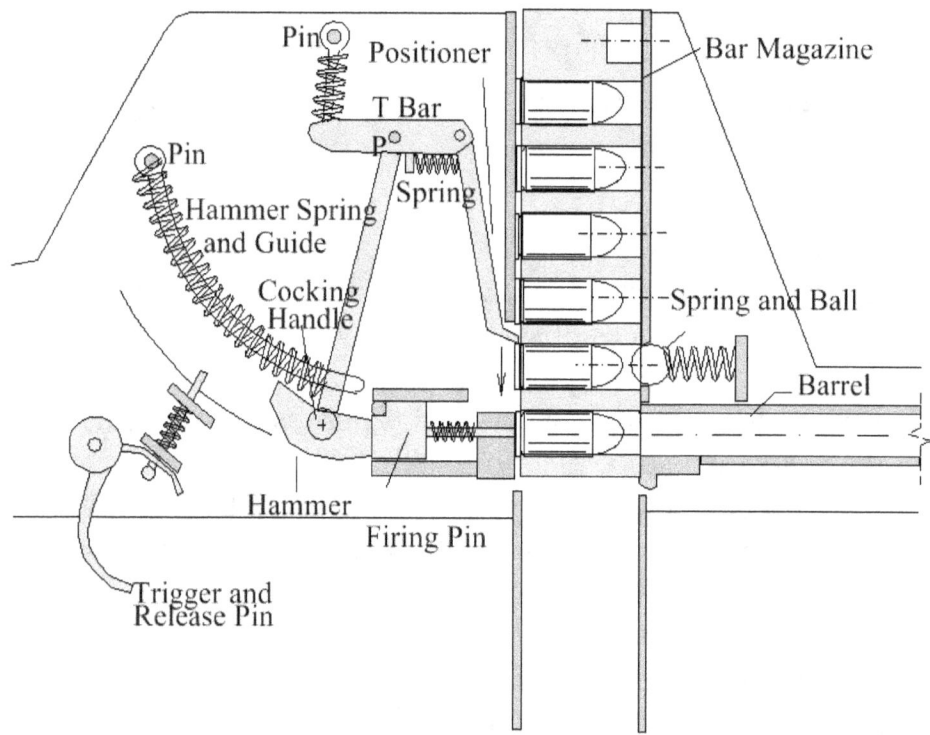

Fig. 8. General Construction View

The block of steel behind the cartridge can be mild steel... it will be substantial though, to handle the forces at the rear of the Bar Magazine, also the thickness front to back will offer a nice guide for the firing pin. The piece of steel that makes up the hammer will be a block of perhaps 1/4" or thicker steel, as will the trigger assembly, but the rest of the inside pieces can be made of 12 or 14 gauge sheet. The two side panels of the receiver can be 14 gauge.

Because the Bar Magazine is thick, 0.90", the outside width of the receiver will be about 1". The "T" Bar unit and Positioner will be thin 12 gauge or 14 gauge, so a piece of steel will run crossways between the receiver side panels to center the T Bar unit; it will actually be **a part** of the T Bar, and will surround and pivot at point "P" and be a critical part to stabilize the T Bar ...at the same time forcing a clean swing without any significant wobble.

Since the Positioner is held against the respective cartridge rim by a spring, it must guide properly to push the Bar Magazine downward during cocking, and then once the gun is fired, it should return to a spot a tad above the next round. Once the final shot is aligned with the barrel and fired, the Positioner must grab the top of the Bar Magazine to eject it after the last shot.

Detailed Bar Magazine Construction

In the last chapter, the boring and basic beginning of the Bar Magazine was described, and at this point more details must be discussed.

I originally wanted to do the Bar Magazine differently. A .45 ACP round does not have a larger diameter rear rim as most cartridges do, it is rimless. In looking at Figure 8, you will note that in the simple mechanism shown, the Positioner must grab the rim of the round for ratcheting the bar through the gun.

This means a method is needed to prevent the round from sliding too far into the Magazine Bar; it must be stopped so that the rim protrudes from the rear of the magazine enough to be caught at each round by the Positioner.

The obvious way to achieve this is by stepping the hole in the Magazine Bar so the forward rim of the cartridge is stopped leaving a precise portion of rim protruding from the rear of the bar. However, this is a very expensive machining process and is difficult in machining the bar!

So what alternatives are available? In the old .45 ACP revolvers, a small C shaped clip was devised called a "Half Moon Clip." Three rounds snapped into the clip and it was used to insert the rounds into the rear of the revolver cylinder and kept them from slipping into the cylinder. Two clips handled six rounds for easy loading.

I thought of two methods for the Bar Magazine:

- In one case, a straight spring clip similar to the Half Moon Clip could be devised for the rear of the Magazine Bar. It could be made of a strip of springy thin steel. It would run down the rear of the bar and would retain the .45 cases to retain the rim in place.

- Another method could use a rim portion of a *fired* .45 Brass case perhaps epoxied into the front of the Bar Magazine; it would form a "step" which would block the cartridge from falling too far into the chamber hole in the bar.

I decided to use the first method as I was concerned about varying lengths of .45 casings and this approach would cover any possibility in cartridge variations. **I recommend this method, it absolutely works and is far less labor intensive than the other approach.**

See Figure 9. This acts as a retainer for the five .45 rounds, gripping the rim slot in each round securely. Any thin, steel would suffice; one possible choice might be heavier pallet strapping. The material should be in approximately 0.90" width.

Each slot must match to each chamber perfectly and be approximately 0.400" wide. It will take a final and very careful grinding with the Dremel tool to do this right; a 3/8" drill can be used initially in the center, spaced 0.700" apart, then use a reamer to enlarge to 0.400. Finally the Dremel can be used to trim to exactly grab each rim as the rounds are in position. This strip should not exceed the width or length of the Bar Magazine when mounted and holding the cartridges.

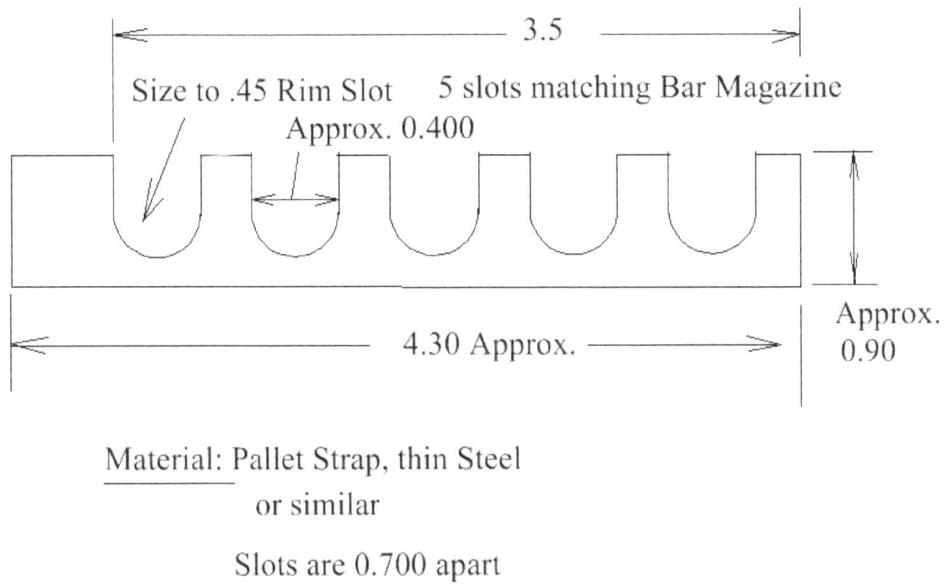

Material: Pallet Strap, thin Steel or similar

Slots are 0.700 apart

Fig. 9. Rim Lock Strip for .45 Cartridges

Test as you do each hole for fitting to the Bar Magazine, the Dremel can do small corrections as the lock strip is tested for fit. Trim to just under the width of the Bar Magazine and close on length as well. A photo of the finished lock strip is shown in Figure 10. Bevel the lower edge of the piece so it will not catch.

I have found that .45 ACP cartridges are quite accurate, which allows using the second method of gluing a portion of Brass cartridge rim into the forward end of the Bar Magazine. This is especially true if a shooting enthusiast uses a particular brand of ammunition like Remington, Winchester or Blazer. It should be possible to do this accurately, then mark and remove any overhang at the front of the bar with a cutoff disk. **One item to**

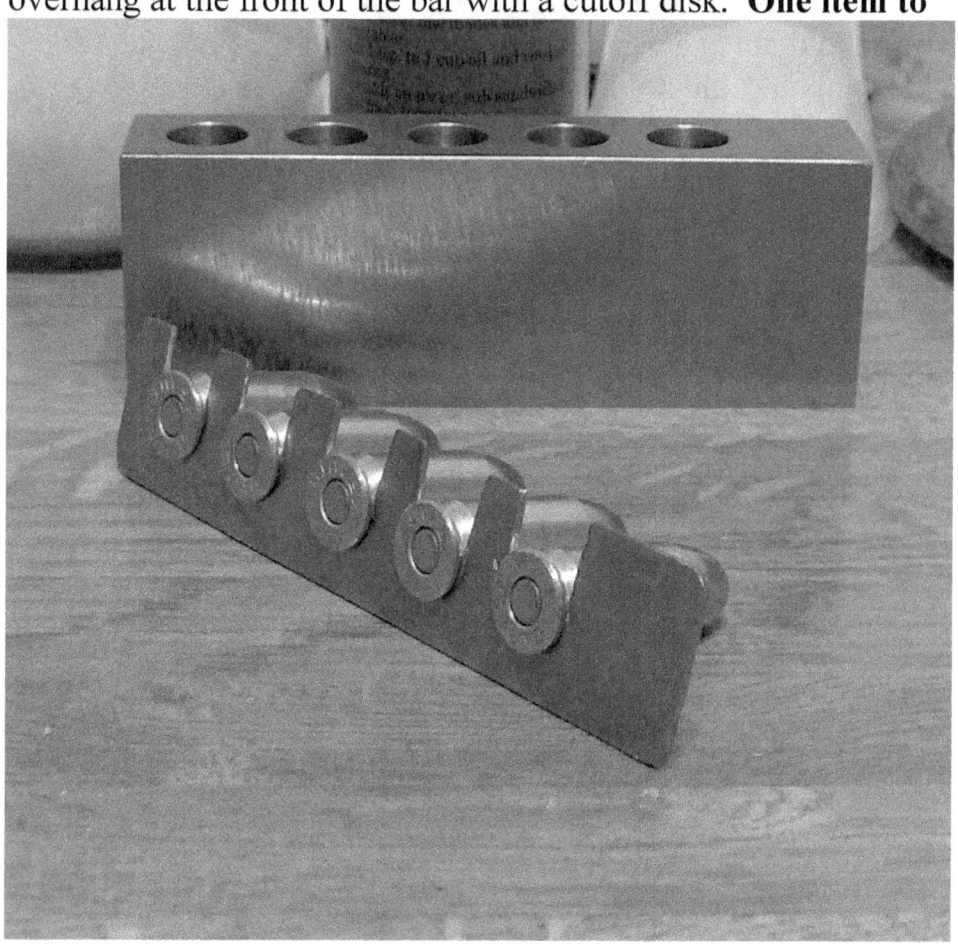

Fig. 10. Finished Rim Lock Strip

note here: the Bar Magazine should be shorter front to rear to do this method. Perhaps 1.25". Because I did not use this method, I cannot vouch for the exact length of usable .45

casing as described.

This is due to the used .45 casings being heavier thickness at the rear. The casing portion glued into the Bar Magazine chamber must be the thin portion only. Any remaining burr can be removed with a grinding bit in a Dremel tool and perhaps a light turn or two of a common tapered hand reamer.

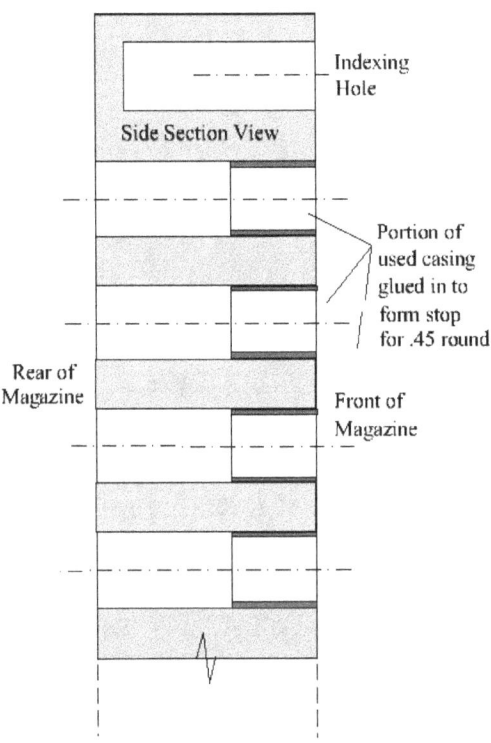

Fig. 11. View of Casing Stops

See Figure 11. Note the simplicity of this method; the portion of Brass "liner" should not be any problem whatsoever. The .45 rim will now be available at the rear of the Bar Magazine for access by the Positioner.

Initially the idea is to place a new .45 round into the rear of the Magazine Bar but use a thin piece of metal or Palette banding as a gauge beneath the rim to prevent it from slipping into the Bar Magazine. The .45 rim should remain outside approximately 1/16 of an inch, at least enough so that the Positioner will grab it reliably.

Then slide a used brass cartridge into the front of the magazine until it contacts the rim of the unfired cartridge. This gives you a rough idea of where to cut off the rim end of the used cartridge.

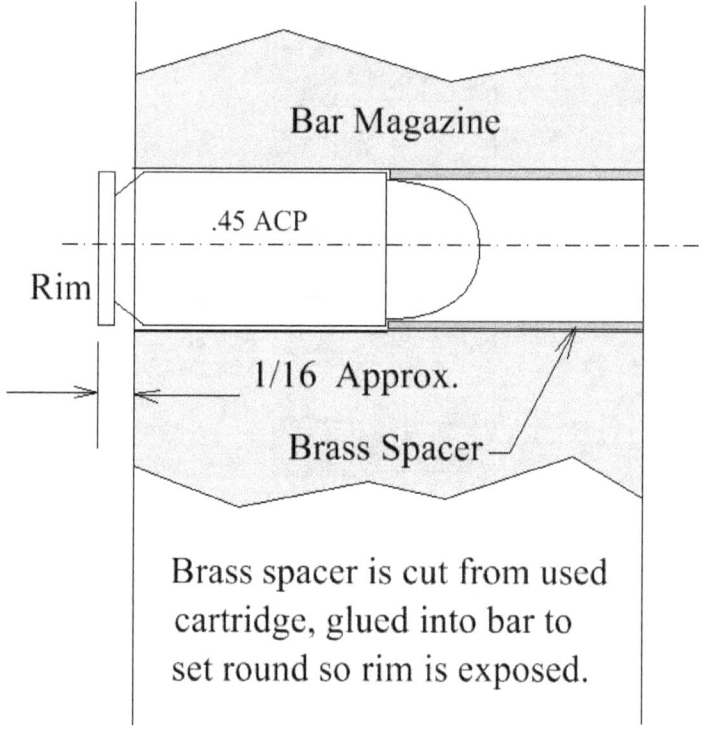

Fig. 12. Detail of Stop

Use a cutoff disk and Dremel tool once you are certain the length is correct. **Wear Safety Glasses, a Dust Mask and perhaps Ear Protection.** Then clean the brass with sandpaper and alcohol, and apply a thin smear of 5 minute epoxy to the outside, and slide it into the chamber hole, maintaining the 1/16 " rim exposure of the good cartridge at the rear of the magazine.

Give it a half hour to dry. This is a very critical part of preparing the magazine, so do it carefully.

Repeat for the remaining four chambers in the magazine, one at a time... make sure all unfired cartridges are spaced so that the rim is protruding identically for all. Be very precise.

This seems to be the simplest method available to do the job. Once this is done and the rim of each round in the magazine inserts so they are identically protruding about 1/16" at the rear of the magazine, the magazine is done.

If during test firing the brass liners appear to be unreliable due to glue failure or whatever, simply revert to the strip form of "Half Moon" clip at the rear of the Bar Magazine described earlier. This gives a reliable alternative to lock the rimless .45 cartridges in place. There are usually some good alternatives for any process.

Items to Order

As we move into the next chapter, it would be a good idea to get some items ahead:

- Be sure to have cutting discs for the Angle Grinder; these are ideal for cutting steel parts.

- Order a Stepless Drill Bit from a tool jobber... Atlas, Northern Tool, this is shown in Chapter 4 Figure 17. It is available from several sources for example Harbor Freight, Item 66463. It is assumed you have standard drill bits up to 1/2" diameter.

- Get the small cutoff discs for a Dremel tool for doing small cutoff jobs, like the slot in the receiver rear guide, etc.

- Be sure you have welding wire, gloves, mask etc. as wire welding will be required for some assembly from Chapter 4 onward.

- **Make sure you have all safety equipment required for the job, dust mask, Face Shield or goggles, and hearing protection!** You will be doing grinding and other dangerous jobs. Be sure you are familiar with each job and the tool for doing it!

Chapter 4

The Receiver

    I drew up some plans and after looking at the diagrams of the gun receiver following, wrote down some approximate sizes needed. The next step was to go to a metal fabricator and ask to check their scrap bin... metal this way is usually very cheap, say 25 cents a lb. I picked out some flat strips of 14 and 12 gauge at least 4" in width, perhaps 2 feet long... usually a strip is long, having been sheared from some job. I also located a small piece of about 1/4" or 3/8" material. It will only take a few small pieces, selected based on the list. Generally, the metal probably will end up costing less than 2 or 3 dollars and will be plenty for the parts needed.

    An Angle Grinder with a cutoff disk cuts steel like butter, and will work perfectly to cut the 14 gauge receiver pieces. This is a dangerous tool unless you are cautious and wear protective items: **Safety Glasses or Face Shield, Dust Mask and Ear Protection**--- and it doesn't hurt to practice on a scrap piece of metal before doing your actual gun part.

    HINT:
When cutting the metal, hold the Angle Grinder very securely, and cut short 2" lengths at a time; this allows very nice straight cuts without losing alignment. Just allow a bit of the disk to penetrate the metal, this makes it easier to adjust the cut.

If you try to cut long stretches, it is easy to get off line. Once cut, it is easy to grind the two pieces to smooth the edge as well as do final shaping as required.

The dimensions in Figure 13 are approximate but having some excess is not a problem as later unnecessary portions may be removed with the Angle grinder. Avoid touching a piece hot from grinding!

A piece of metal cut with the Angle Grinder will have very sharp metal filaments at the cut edge, be very careful of these and remove them before handling those edges!

Once the two pieces are cut, it is a good idea to grind the portions at the front to match... the front part shape will likely be fairly firm, the rear portion is more likely to be modified later.

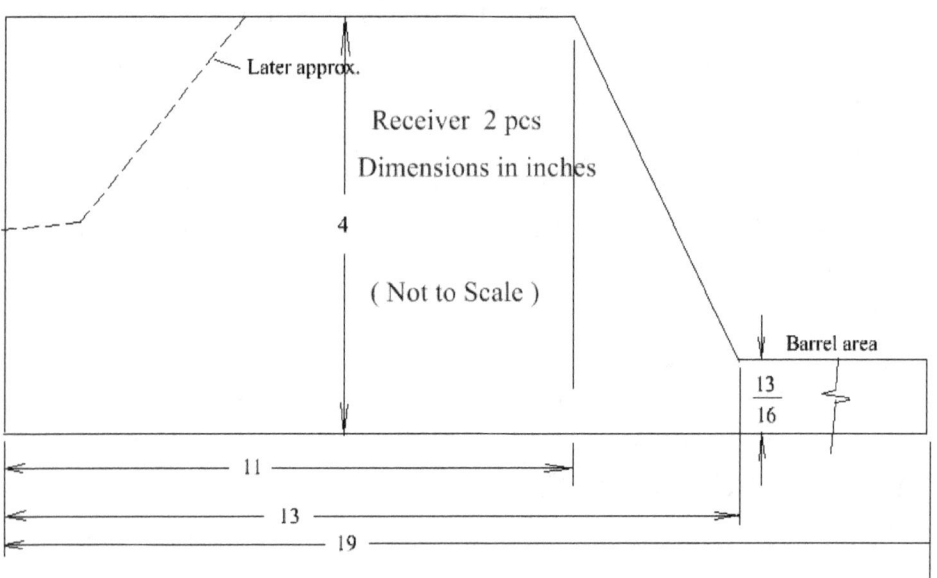

Fig. 13. Receiver Panels

A photo of the cut panels is shown in Figure 14. Note the

piece is fairly true, cutting in small lengths with the Angle Grinder allows good control. Note the safety wear in the photo, **Don't cut corners on Safety!** Always think through each job before you do it.

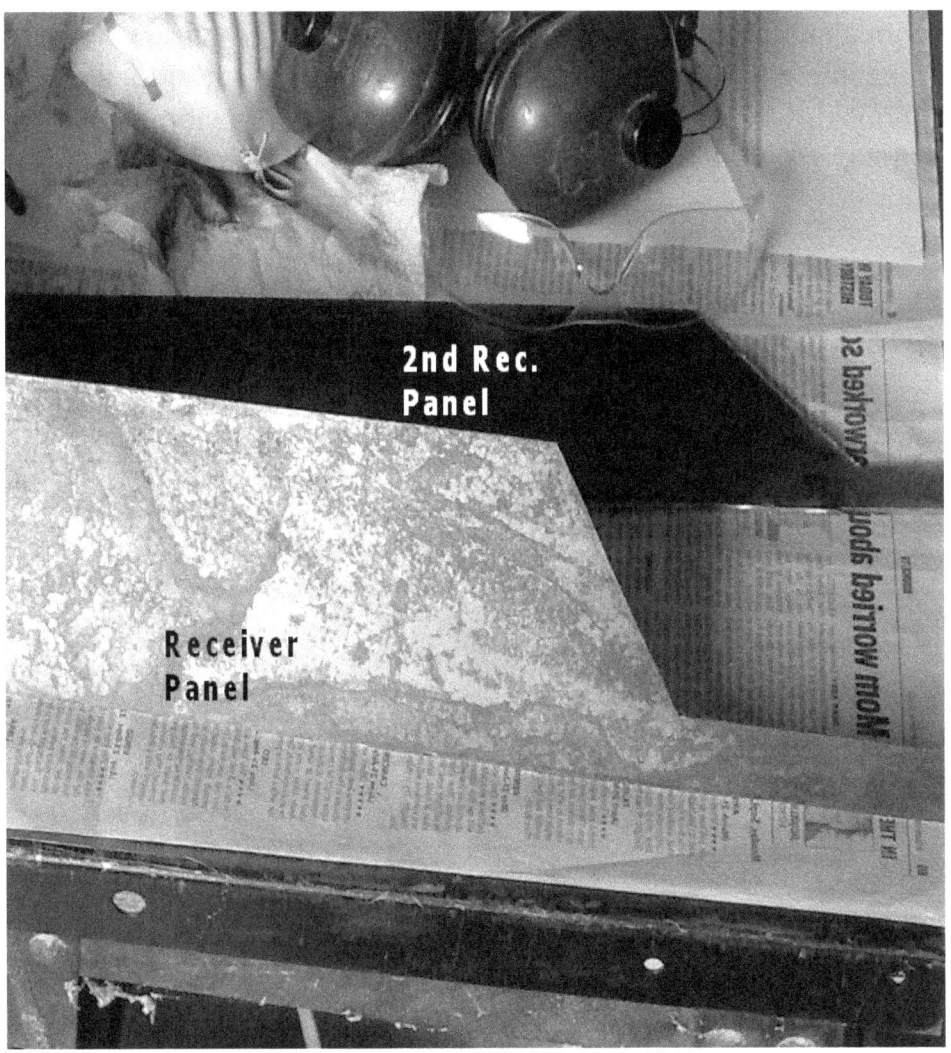

Fig. 14. Photo of Rough Receiver Panels

Front Bar Magazine Guide

The next part of the job is to cut the front guide for the Bar Magazine. This part must be carefully ground to a perfect fit to allow the Bar Magazine to slide down through the gun with no sloppiness; afterward the hole for the ball detent and barrel must be precisely centered so that when the barrel is mounted, the Bar Magazine will index correctly for perfect alignment of the barrel. Obviously a slow careful job is required, otherwise it must be redone.

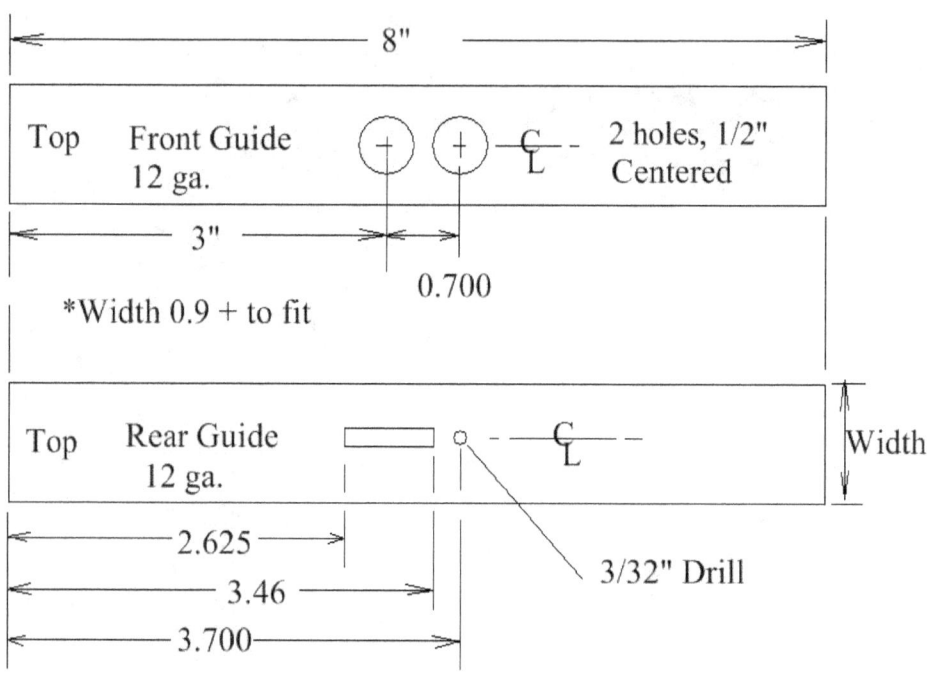

Fig. 15. Front and Rear Bar Magazine Guides

See Figure 15 which shows both the front and rear Bar Magazine guides.
Initially my front guide was thinner and during test firing in Chapter 12, the guide bulged inward, grabbing the Bar

Magazine. Going to 12 gauge steel fixed this problem.

The rear guide will be reinforced by a substantial steel block immediately behind the cartridge that is aligned with the firing pin. The slot above the firing pin hole is for the Positioner to move the magazine assembly.

These two pieces will mount on one receiver panel, welded or fastened with brackets. The other receiver side is the removable side for maintenance and servicing the rifle.

The front guide will be mounted right at the 11 inch point where the receiver panel angles down towards the barrel support. The top of the guide should be adjusted so the barrel hole and the bottom surface of the barrel will essentially lie even with the bottom of the receiver piece barrel support arm.

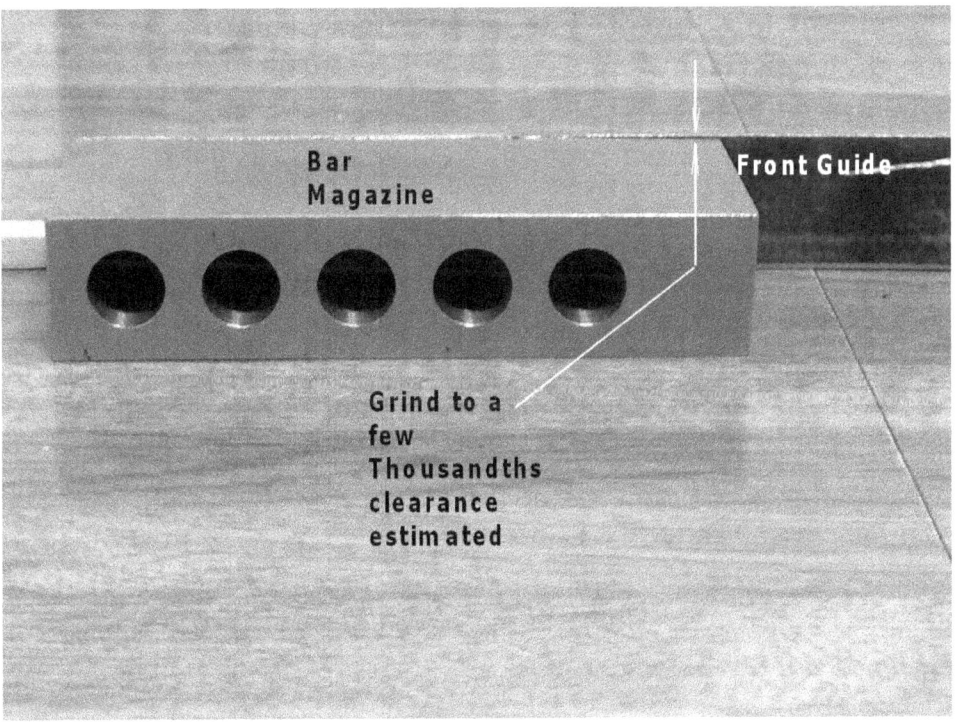

Fig. 16. Magazine Clearance of Magazine Guides

Careful fitting as the piece is made will assure a good alignment. Grind the front guide width cautiously after cutting to maintain only a few thousandths spacing for the Bar Magazine. See Figure 16 and note the minimal front guide allowance space for magazine clearance... you can just see the shine of the edge of the front guide above the magazine.... this is most critical at the area surrounding the barrel and ball detent, down near the bottom of the magazine guide a bit more clearance is not a problem. As you sight across the magazine laying in place on the one receiver panel the front guide should just be visible above the magazine with an extremely minimal clearance.

The Ball Detent and Barrel Holes

Carefully drill the two holes as shown in Figure 14. Inspect the two holes you drill in the front guide for the ball detent and the barrel. Align them to two holes in the Bar Magazine. A slight spacing error *between* holes can be fixed as long as the ball detent hole is centered. That is the critical point, because the barrel opening hole can simply be enlarged later with no harm. It is only required to allow the bullet to pass through, it does nothing else. What is critical is the ball detent locking the Bar Magazine in position for a bullet to pass correctly into the barrel.

The Ball Detent hole should be fitted prior to any welding of the front guide …. the idea is to have a significant portion of the 9/16" ball inside the magazine area to grab the magazine very securely. You can perhaps enlarge the 1/2" detent ball hole using a hand reamer. But you must be able to go larger than 1/2" diameter. Or use the reamer looking Stepless Drill Bits similar to Harbor Freight's part no. 66463. See Figure 17. This type bit is typically available from several tool sources. Drill gently to enlarge the ball detent hole a bit at a time, and check after each incremental drilling with the Bar Magazine and detent ball placed in the guide hole until it just locks the Bar Magazine firmly when the ball is held in place. The ball <u>must not be sloppy</u> in the front guide, and it must also fit into the Bar Magazine with a firm lock allowing <u>no movement</u>.

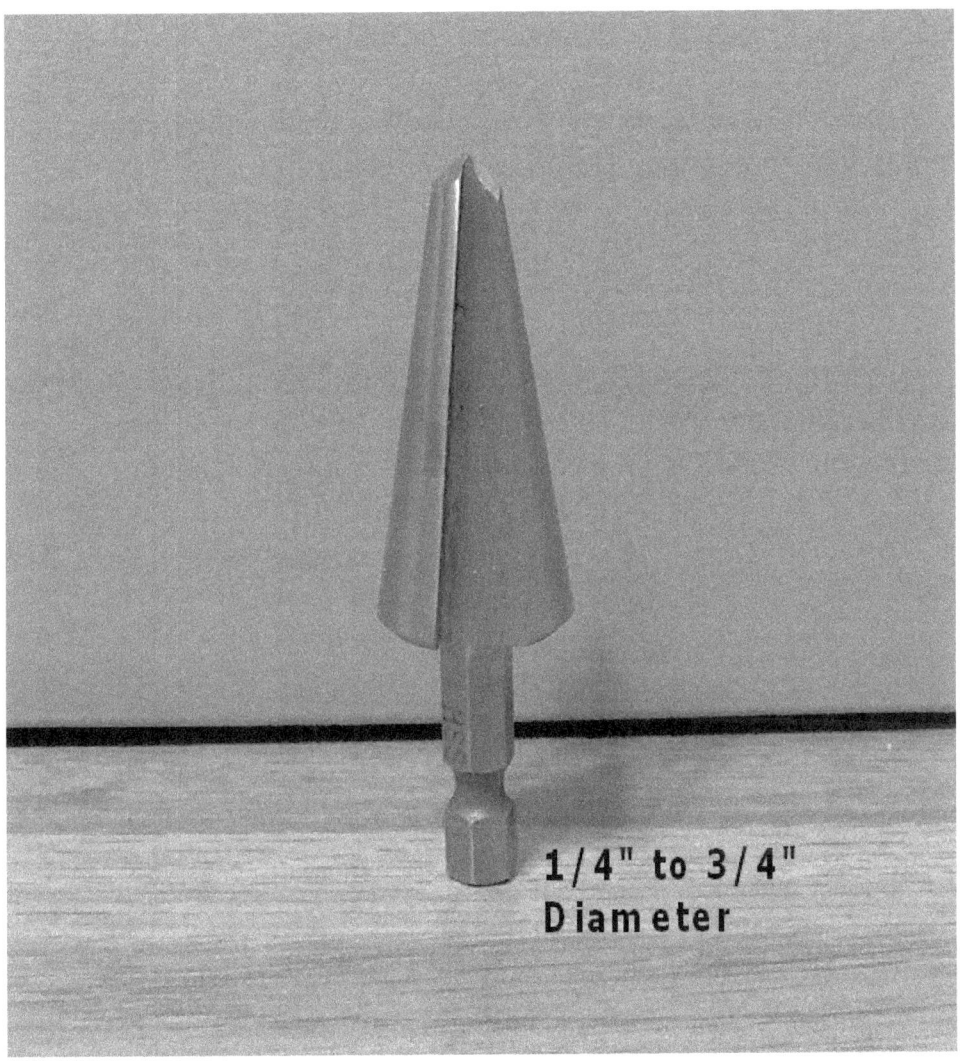

Fig. 17. Stepless Drill Bit

When testing, the Bar Magazine must have no slop whatsoever along its long axis when held by the ball as it slides against the guide. Cross-wise slop is not as critical since the guide widths restrain side slop in the magazine slot. If you drill slightly too much, use a punch to ping the edge of the hole slightly, maybe 3 spots equally around the circumference.

Once satisfied with the detent hole configuration and the lock effect, you are ready to enlarge the barrel hole as well to about 9/16" if necessary. Grind or ream as needed.

After you have these two holes ready you are almost ready to mount the front guide. Before any welding, apply a piece of Masking Tape over these two holes to protect from weld spatter.

Front Guide Install

Once you have carefully drilled, filed and sized the front guide to your satisfaction, put a slight forward bend in the upper quarter inch to allow an easy entry for the Bar Magazine.

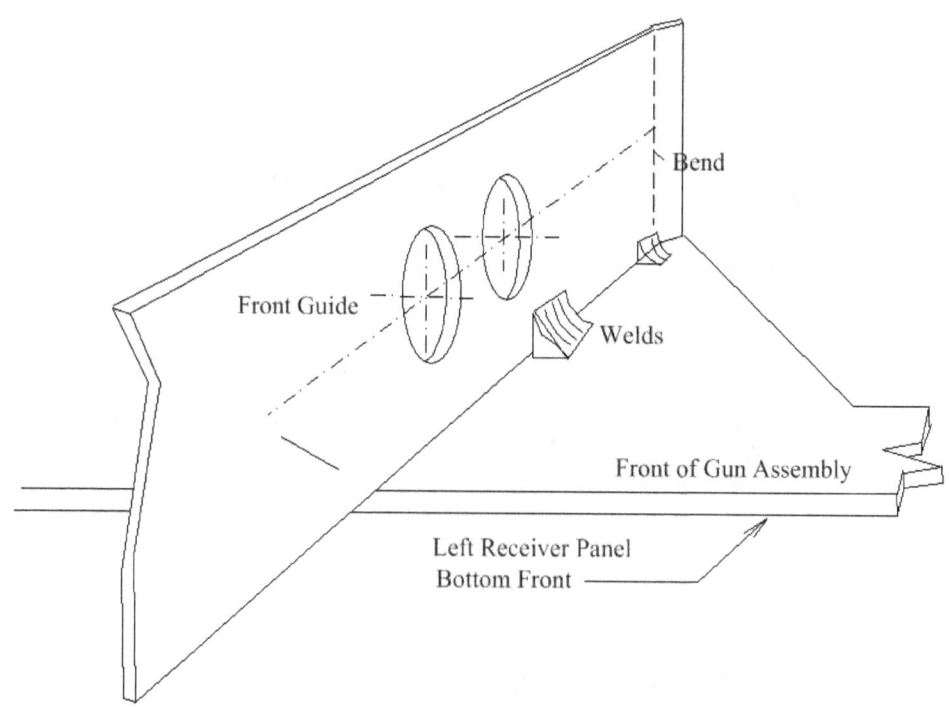

Fig 18. Detail Front Guide Mounting

Then use a squared steel piece to clamp it perfectly vertical to the receiver on edge as shown in Figure 18, right at the 11 inch angle cut. Weld it to the left receiver (or alternatively, weld mounting brackets onto it as you prefer...) Use a piece of angle iron or something similar to clamp the front guide vertically in place and perpendicular to the lower edge of the receiver. Do some practice welding to set the wire speed on your wire welder. A little practice on some scraps should build confidence.

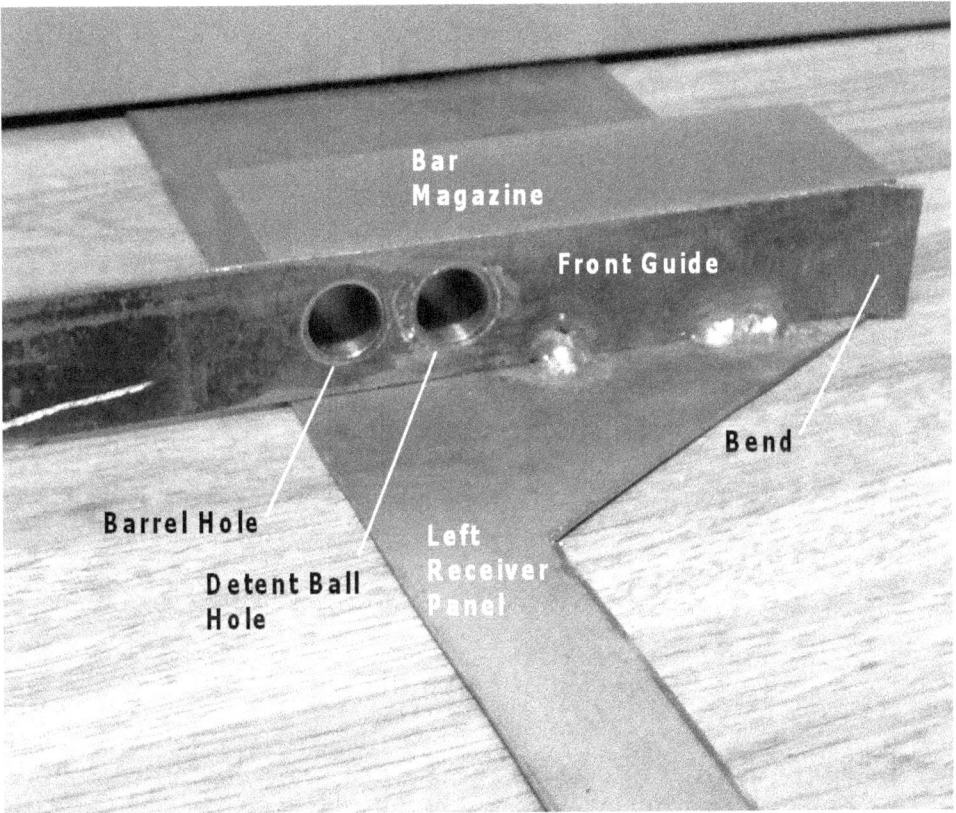

Fig. 19. Photo of Front Guide Welded

It is desired to be perfectly vertical when finished. As you weld, only weld a couple of short fillets; that is all that is required and true the front guide vertically as you do. Do not block the area around the two 1/2" holes with welding, you will need to place a guide for the ball detent setup there. Weld above that area to avoid any interference. Clean off any weld spatter and beads. See Figure 19.

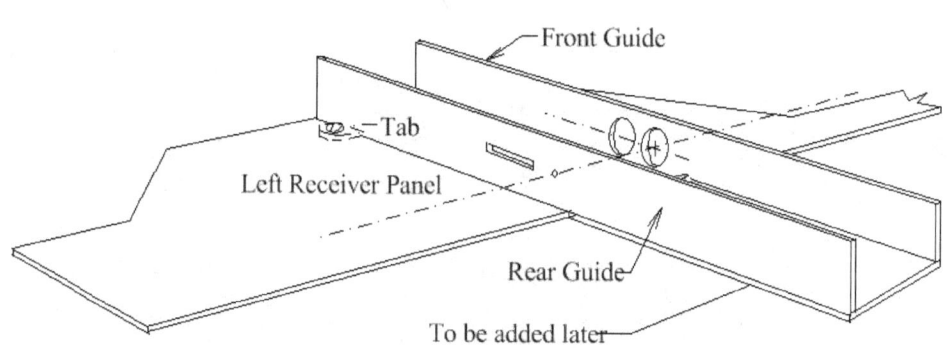

Fig. 20. Mounting Rear Guide

The Rear Guide

The slot in the rear guide is done by drilling a hole at each end of the location show in Figure 15 and perhaps in between. with a 1/8" bit, then using a Dremel tool with cutting disk to cut the metal out between. A bit of filing will finalize it so the 12 or 14 gauge Positioner will access nicely to grab the .45 cartridge rims.

Because the rear guide should be adjustable until the fit to the Bar Magazine is completed, I welded a tab for mounting onto the side of the guide up near the top of the piece. I drilled the tab for a 6-32 clearance. It may be a good idea to add another later, but the plan is for the block at the rear of the Bar Magazine chamber to be that other support. See Figure 20 and 21. **Do not weld the rear guide onto the receiver panel,** only drill to mount using the screw tab that is welded near the top of the rear guide! We will be doing several critical adjustments and checks to be sure we get it into the correct spot and have the Positioner slot tweaked for proper operation.

Fig. 21. Rear Guide Setup

Drill the receiver panel to align the rear guide so that the firing pin hole matches to the center of the barrel hole in the front guide. Mount the rear guide using the screw tab and a 6-32 screw. It can easily be removed for finishing touches as we weld a reinforcing breech block and check Positioner operation, etc.

At this point, you should order the 9/16" ball and some compression springs. Any hardware store with the extensive parts bins will usually have an assortment of excellent springs. Also, Amazon.com carries a slew of compression springs in all different diameters and lengths; based on my experience with the previous .22 rifle in "Homebuilt Firearms", certainly you can order springs there.

- 9/16" Steel ball from Bearingballstore.com or another industrial source.

- Compression Springs, packages are available from Amazon.com, Grainger and other hardware sources. Remember, some good hardware stores carry bins and assorted springs. Springs of 0.300 to 7/16" diameter and 0.042 to 0.048 wire size 3 inches long are probably good for the stronger springs for the hammer and a similar shorter spring for the ball detent mechanism.
- Amazon is a vendor for springs from: Reid Supply Co., www.ReidSupply.com, and Small Parts, Inc.

- A lighter spring should be fine for the upper return spring on the "T" Bar, the Positioner Spring, hammer release and a firing pin spring... like something from Ace Hardware Compression Springs Assortment 5213517.

Chapter 5

T Bar and Positioner

Next comes the "T" Bar and Positioner mechanism. These parts form the rotating support assembly for the hammer and also the setup to move the Bar Magazine one round at a time through the rifle.

The construction is very important, taking into particular consideration the spacing between rounds, so the Positioner will not move lower than required to set the Bar Magazine in place for the ball detent to perfectly catch and lock the magazine.

The lower position must be correct to put a round in line with the barrel., the upper position allows the Positioner to go *above the rim of the next round,* far enough to also grab the empty magazine after the last shot and eject the magazine.

This gives the basic information for setting up the position and sizing of the "T" at the top, and its geometry to achieve this at the same time as the cocking motion for firing a cartridge.

From my experience with the .22 build in "Homebuilt Firearms," it takes about 40 to 45 degrees angle of rotation for the cocking motion with typical springs I found in order to assure sufficient spring force to fire a cartridge. This is just a rough rule of thumb essentially... but gives a good basis for starting the calculations. Additionally, the design shown sets correct operation even as the angle goes to 45 degrees. This gives a huge allowance for setting up the hammer cocking springs later on.

The first thing to recognize is that as the arm rotates, at the lowest Positioner location, the Positioner and the "T" arm it is attached to should be essentially limited from further movement. At this point, the Ball Detent should have grabbed the Bar Magazine and locked it into place. Study Figure 22.

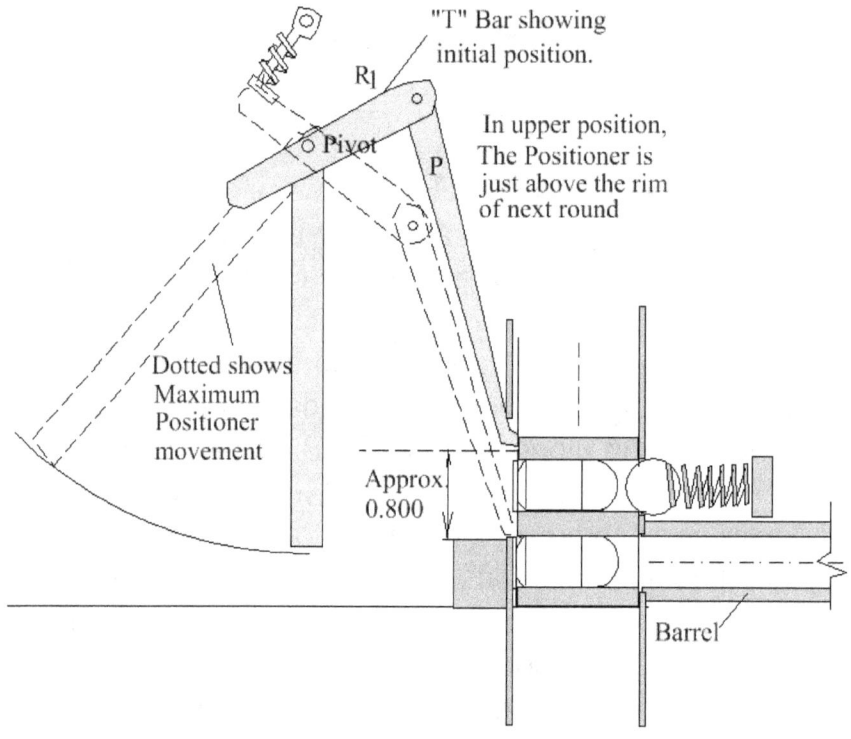

Fig. 22. Simplified View of "T" Bar and Positioner

This geometry requires that the "T" Bar not be a perfect "T". The upper crosspiece will be tilted somewhat on both sides to meet the desired conditions with the Positioner on the right, and to allow a compression return spring on the top of the left crossbar. The lengths are not accurate in the figure however the principle is clearly shown. Some calculations will get the setup into the ball park, and a final fit will be done with the actual receiver assembly.

At the rest position with the "T" Bar positioned to allow the Positioner to grab the next round; we still have the distance between rounds at 0.700", plus the Positioner should lie perhaps 0.100" above the rim of the next round to be moved down. That comes to approximately 0.800 of movement.

Looking at the geometry... if we split the angle that the right arm of the "T" Bar moves fairly evenly about the horizontal, it accomplishes two things:

- The closer the Positioner is to the rear guide, the better the alignment force to push the Bar Magazine down. By keeping the rotation arc close to the rear guide, this criterion is held. If the arc is split approximately equal above and below horizontal in the figure, the distance is a minimum. (The Positioner will be closer to the guide during its major motion...) With the tab mounting for the rear guide, I allowed a 3/4" space between the guide and the rightmost end of the "T" arm.

- This insures a fairly parallel position for the initial and final location of the Positioner. This will make it easier for the Positioner spring to apply a nice even pressure through the main movement cycle. This setup means the left end of the Positioner attached to the "T" arm will be essentially an equal distance start and finish from the rear of the Bar Magazine. It means the vertical movement desired of about 0.800 will be the same as the vertical movement of the "T" arm/Positioner pinned point.

Look at Figure 23. This lays out the two principles above, and allows a mathematical check. Study the diagram carefully. You will see two triangles, one ABC, which represents the starting point prior to moving the Bar Magazine... and the other, abc representing the position after movement.

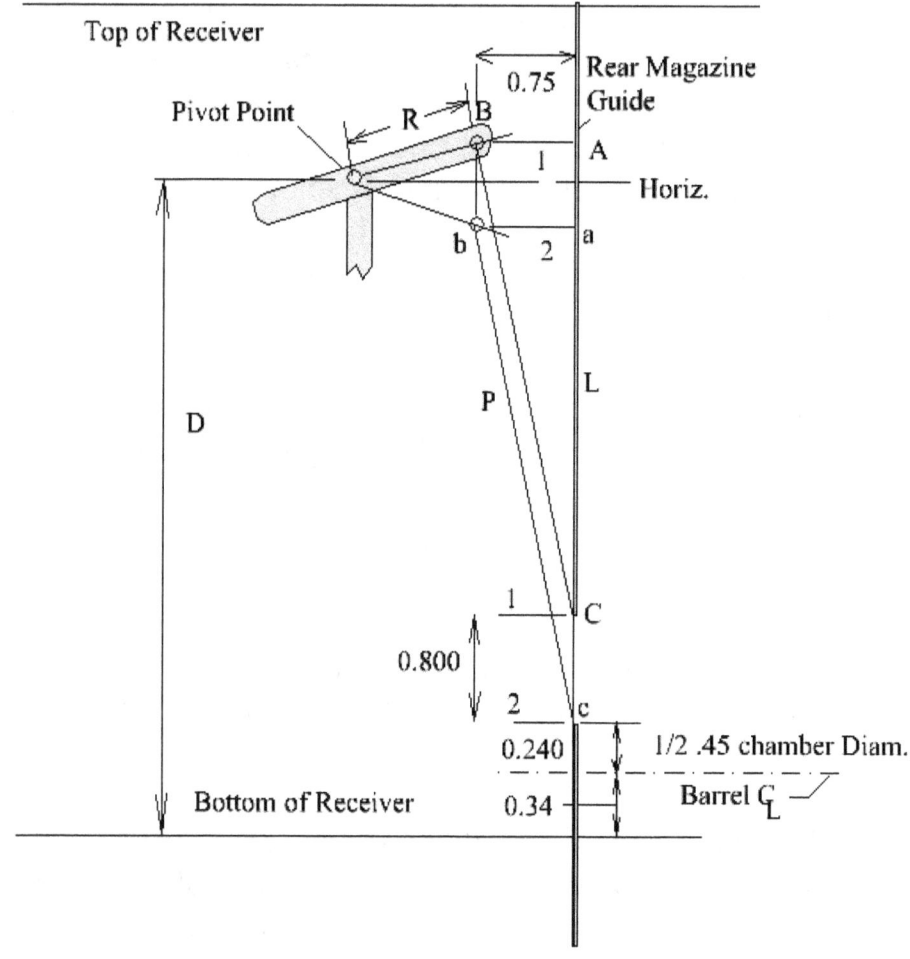

Fig. 23. Diagram for Calculations

With an equal movement above and below the horizontal, the start and end points of the "T" arm are B and b, and the two triangles are identical. L is identical so using this:

For ABC L = D + (R sinx) - (0.800 + 0.240 + 0.34)

For abc L = D − (R sinx) - (0.34 + 0.240)

Then (R sinx) - (1.38) = - (R sinx) - (0.58)

So 2(R sinx) = (1.38 - .58) = 0.80 (see the match...)

Assume say 20 degrees above and below for a total of 40 degrees "T" Bar rotation. This will give a ballpark for the radius of the right "T" arm:

R = 0.40/ 0.342 = 1.18"

This gives us a good estimate for the right arm radius. Approximately 1.2" .

Next we need to get the Positioner length. Wishing to place a return spring on the left "T" arm, lets allow 1" from the top of the receiver.... this gives D = 3". Substituting and using the 20 degree angle:

L = 3 − (1.18 x Sinx) - (0.58)   or

L = 3 - (1.18 x 0.342) − 0.58 = 2.02"

Tangent Angle C = 0.75/ 2.02 = 0.371

Angle C = 20.4 degrees

P (Cos 20.4 degrees) = L = 2.02

P = 2.02/ 0.937 = 2.16"

These values give a good starting point, and can be adjusted during construction.

See Figure 24, which shows a general construction of the "T" Bar.

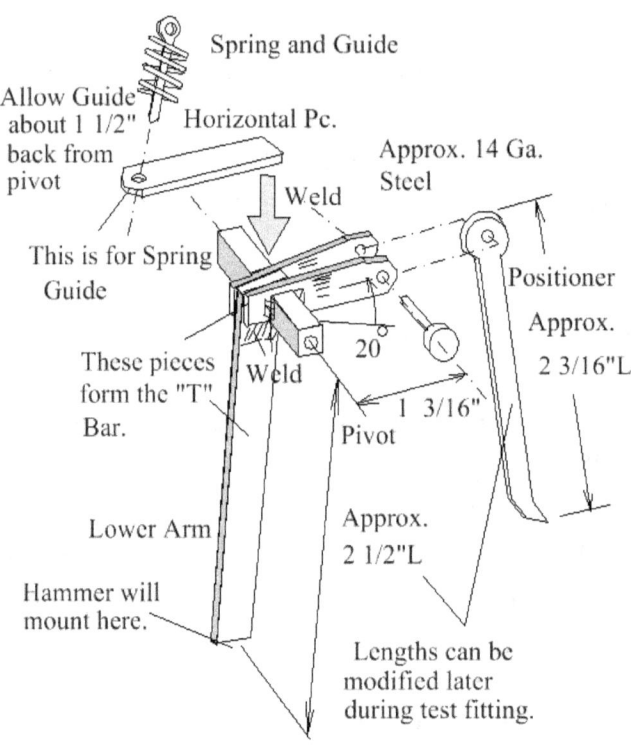

Fig. 24. General Build of "T" Bar

Basically in building this part, we follow the general dimensions we calculated above except leave a bit extra length on the lower arm, horizontal piece and the Positioner. Do not drill the holes for attaching the Positioner. Later as you test the positioning and operation, you can adjust the hole and round the right arm to give a neat appearance. See Figure 25.

The right arm is made of two pieces, which sandwich on each side of the lower "T" arm, and are bent slightly to form a clevis

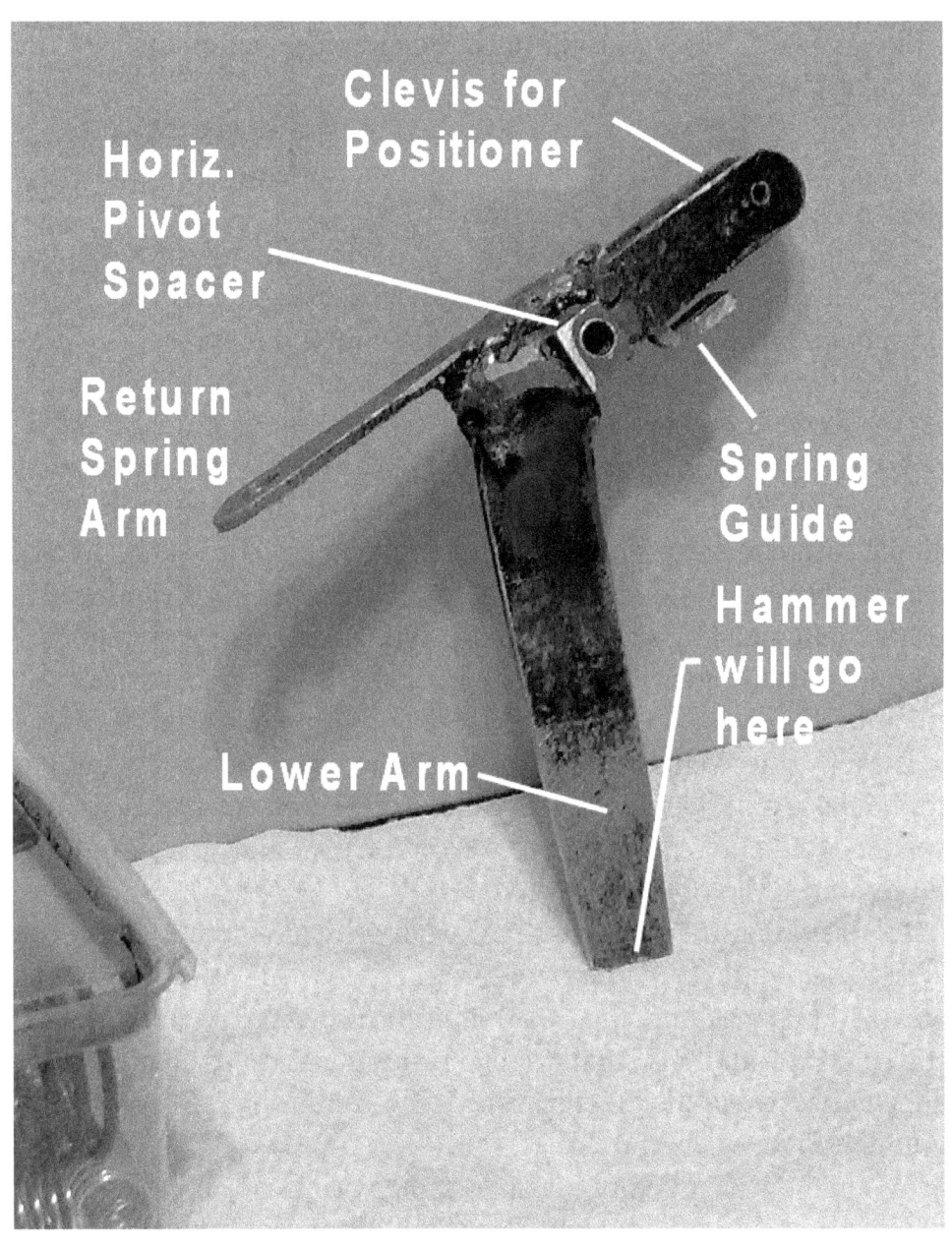

Fig. 25. Actual "T" Bar Assembly

over the top of the Positioner. Angle the right arm pieces about 20 degrees upward (CCW) from perpendicular to the lower arm.

This establishes the approximate 20 degree as used in the calculations of Figure 23.

Welding these small pieces with a wire welder is tricky, requires care and wearing proper equipment, and, as always... **plan ahead with a mind to safety.**

Clamp and weld the two clevis pieces onto the top of the lower arm. Clean off the weld spatter and beads. Then weld the horizontal piece onto the top of the assembly.

Finally, cut two pieces of 1/4" x 1/4" Steel of about 3/8" length to weld onto each side of the "T" assembly at the pivot point; this forms the horizontal pivot spacer between the receiver side panels. Or use the angle grinder to cut a slot to mount a single full piece across and integral to the cross arm. This pivot spacer eliminates side play and helps center the "T" piece for proper hammer impact on the firing pin. Because of the welds already present, you will need to grind these two pieces carefully to mount for a nice centered horizontal alignment of the "T" Bar. It is tricky, the welds will probably not be beautiful as it is hard to see these small areas as you weld... do your best, and clean off spatter beads, etc. You can use a Dremel Tool and small grinding bit to dress it up once fabricated.

At this point, there is one small-- but critical-- item to add. There is a small spring that will mount on the "T" assembly clevis to press against the Positioner during engagement with the rim of each round. A small metal spring guide must be made and attached between the clevice arms to hold this spring. Note this guide in Figures 25 and 26.

When the "T" assembly is at rest, the spring will press against the Positioner lightly, but sufficient to hold it securely in the rear guide slot to grab the cartridge rim. As the "T" Bar rotates, and at the lowest Positioner point, with the cartridge grabbed in position for firing, the spring force is much less, due to rotation of the "T" Bar creating a greater space between the bar and Positioner. This is important, because on hammer release, there should be minimal friction contact as the Positioner slides back up into the rest or start position. The hammer must swing freely to fire the round.

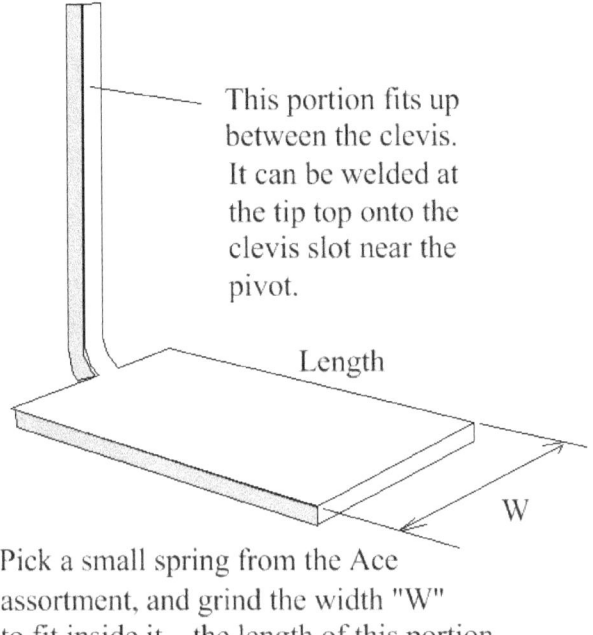

This portion fits up between the clevis. It can be welded at the tip top onto the clevis slot near the pivot.

Length

W

Pick a small spring from the Ace assortment, and grind the width "W" to fit inside it.. the length of this portion should be a bit shorter than the spring when the "T" bar is at the rest position .

Fig. 26. Positioner Spring Guide

Later, when the hammer is added, the lower arm will be set up with a slot for the hammer spring guide.

If two angle pieces are made to encompass the detent spring and ball, that portion can also be done now to give a more complete start for the receiver and the internal mechanism to allow testing.

Some boss spacers can also be welded onto one receiver panel, then drilled and tapped, or drilled clearance to allow for joining of the receiver panels. Aligning the receiver panels is a good idea for some of the drilling and placement.

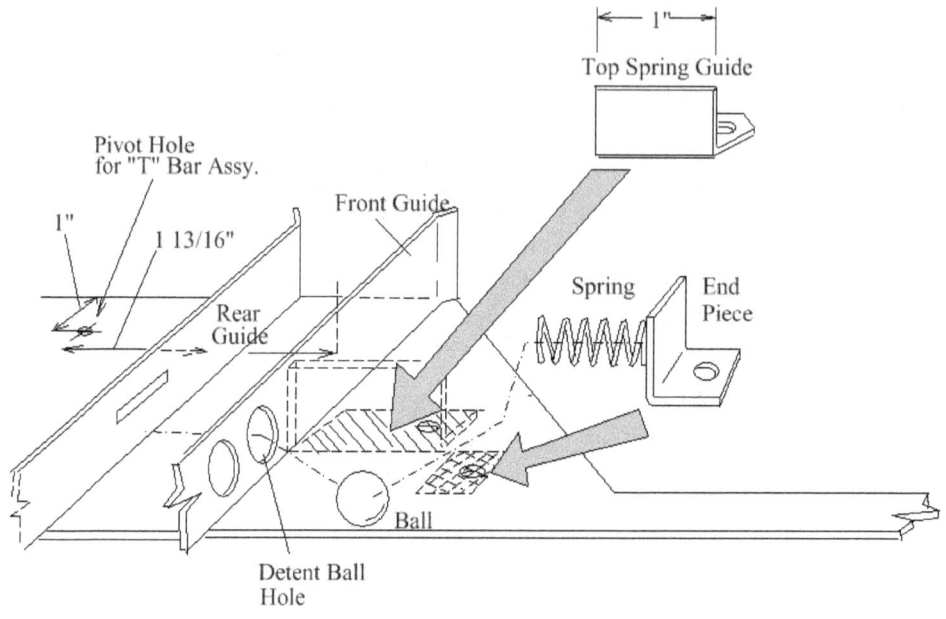

Fig. 27. Ball Detent Housing

Also one boss should mount above the "T" Bar clevis as a stop to prevent over travel in the counter-clockwise direction at the rest position. If the bar rotates too far CCW, the Positioner will come out of the slot in the rear magazine guide. At some point, the head of the long screw that the "T" Bar pivots upon can also be welded on the outside of the receiver while the receiver is bolted together and aligned true.

Starting the Build

Make the two "L" brackets shown in Figure 27 to house the detent ball and spring. The two brackets should stand a bit less than the height of the magazine guides. The barrel will mount below the spring to form a lower limit. A piece of 14 gauge steel will be welded between the barrel and ball detent chamber to enclose the mechanism.

Position them to allow the ball detent and spring to function and determine the mounting position. For now they can be mounted with screws. Later on, if satisfactory, they can be welded if desired. There is a 1/2"x 1" approx. spring in the Ace Spring assortment that is ideal for initial testing and setup of the ball detent.

Next mark a position 1" below the top edge of the receiver and 1 13/16" behind the rear magazine guide and drill a 6-32 clearance hole in the left panel for the pivot of the "T" Bar assembly. Use a long 1 1/2" screw up through the hole as the pivot screw.

See Figure 28. The detent spring is a weaker version for testing, the bosses have not been installed, etc. but it gives an idea of progress thus far! In operating the mechanism, it becomes obvious which critical items are needed:

- the stop is needed above the clevis on the right "T" Arm.

- The final detent spring must be fairly strong to grab the Bar Magazine. *Also a centering guide or something similar should be added later to keep the spring axially aligned with the ball. This is merely a centered dowel through the end piece to hold the spring in straight alignment with the ball.*

- Also as the magazine ratchets through, a second lock should be there to firmly grab each round. With such a heavy Bar Magazine to hold .45 ACP rounds, it is conceivable that the bar might lose grab and click right through the gun! This will be discussed later.

Testing the Mechanism

It is a good time to test the function of the Positioner, and the rest of the mechanism. Place the bar magazine with some rounds locked into the rim clip carefully into the slot between the magazine guide.

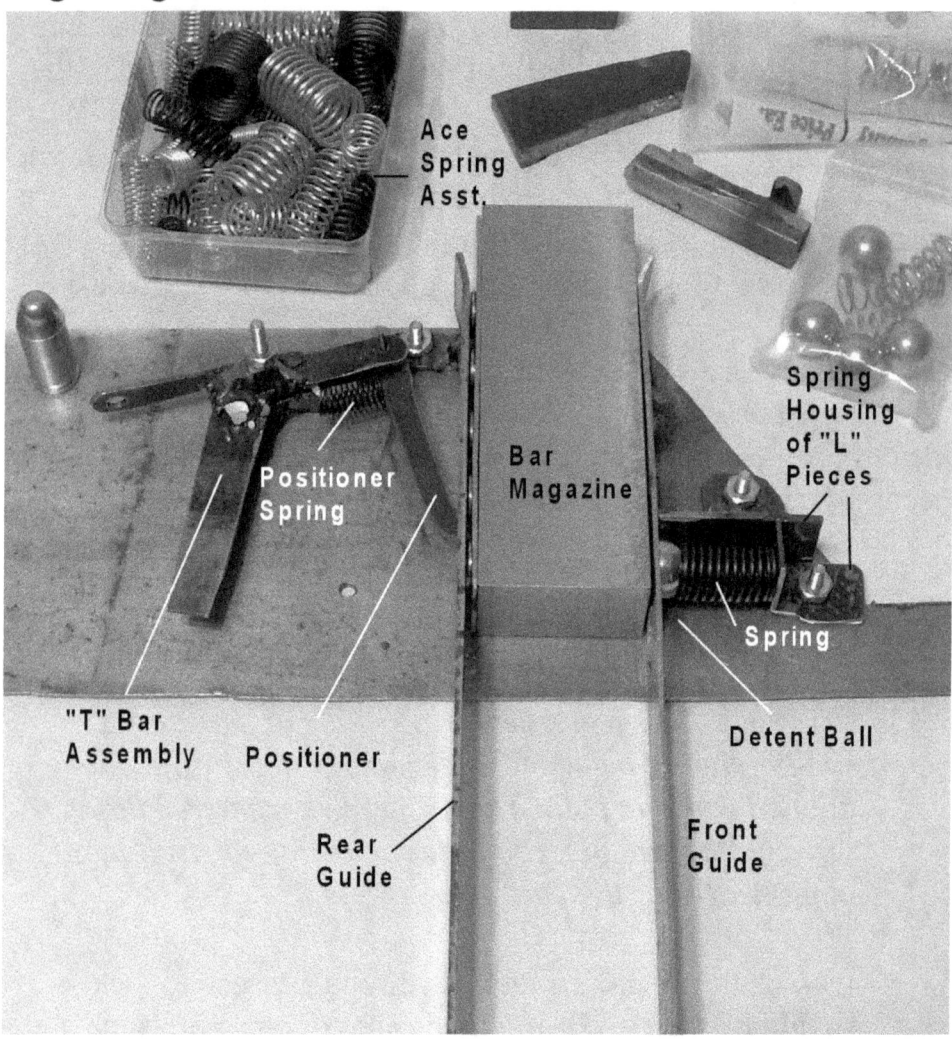

Fig. 28. Testing the Setup

Push it down until the first hole in the front is grabbed by the detent ball. Keeping the receiver flat on the worktable, operate the "T" Bar from an approximate rest position with the lower arm approximately straight down towards the bottom of the receiver panel. Figure 28 shows this configuration, and parts mounting of the present build.

Rotate the "T" Bar assembly clockwise and check that the Positioner ratchets the bar Magazine down one round and the ball detent grabs the respective hole, aligning the chamber below with the barrel hole. Carefully grind the Positioner tip if necessary to get perfect operation. You should be able to ratchet the magazine down and eventually out of the barrel position.

Rotate the "T" Bar back so the Positioner resets and grabs another round at the top of the Positioner slot between each ratcheting action. Grind and lengthen the slot slightly if needed.

Once you are satisfied, it is time to move to the hammer and firing pin construction in the next chapter.

The spacer boss should be mounted above the right arm of the "T" assembly to block CCW rotation of the "T" Arm so it can't rotate so far as to bring the Positioner out of the guide slot at the top point of motion. The spacer should also be a height to set correct spacing between the receiver panels. It can be drilled and tapped or drilled clearance, and it should be welded vertically to the one receiver panel.

Be sure the rear guide piece is removable to add reinforcing, and to drill further as required; <u>it must not be permanently attached yet to the receiver panel.</u> That comes later.

Later on, the "T" Bar lower arm will also be reinforced to resist against the twisting component of force during cocking.

Chapter 6

Hammer and Firing Pin Assembly

After building the "T" Bar piece, and the receiver portions, the firing pin and block behind the cartridge and barrel should be made. These parts are important to interface with the "T" Bar, in particular the hammer which impacts directly on the firing pin assembly. With the Bar Magazine and rear guide set in place, it will be obvious where mounting should be for the firing pin and block support.

Before doing the firing pin, the area of the rear guide right behind the cartridge needs to be reinforced by adding a thick steel pad, which will later be welded onto the one receiver. I believe an equivalent 1/2" thick steel block will suffice and it will also be welded to the rear guide. Remove the rear magazine guide and weld the block onto the rear guide so that the block is aligned at the bottom of the Positioner slot. It can be sandwiched 1/4" material or solid. It should be about 5/8" wide x 3/4" high. Clean off the weld and bead spatter.

Caution....Do not weld the rear guide to the receiver until all drilling and welding is finished on the rear guide. Be patient, still a few steps to go.

Next, turn the rear magazine guide over and use the existing firing pin hole as a guide to drill through the block you have

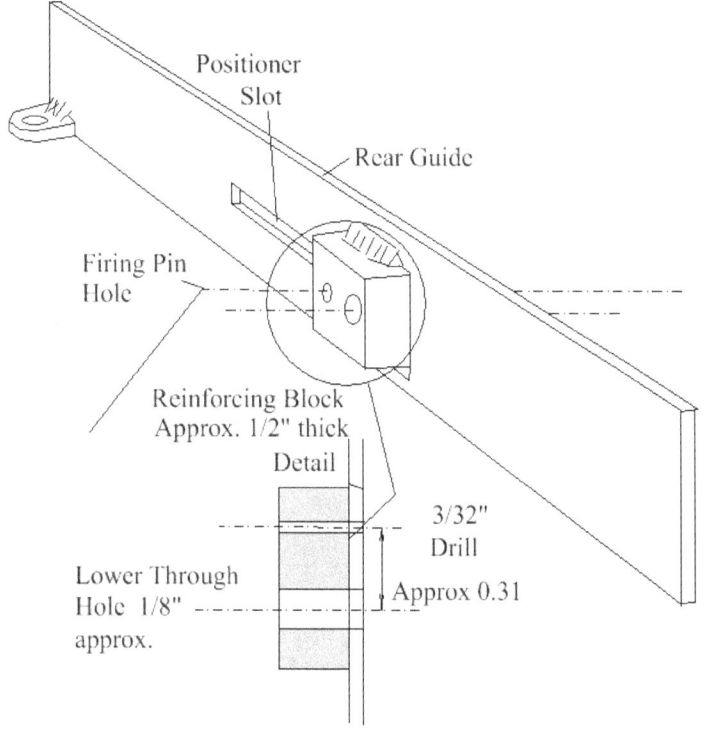

Fig. 29. Support Block, Other Details

mounted onto the rear guide. Use plenty of oil for lube, and drill only a small depth at a time. Remember in tightening the chuck to use all three chuck holes and gradually tighten the chuck.

The end of the firing pin will be surface hardened later, or in fact, <u>you could use a 3/32" drill bit as the firing pin.</u> That is a good choice as well; drill bits are extremely strong and hard.

In my case I had gotten in a hurry and welded the rear guide onto the receiver, so I had a 3/32" hole and was thinking of using a drill bit as the actual firing pin. I had drilled the other lock pin hole too, so was prepared in that sense. But had I not got in a hurry, I would have had more options.

The other hole is done to provide a positive lock pin to insure a reliable catch to augment the ball detent... the chamber MUST NOT advance past alignment with the barrel, it must lock into perfect alignment every time. **The lock pin hole must be drilled and centered below the firing pin hole and a tad past half diameter of a .45 rim away.** Mark the distance; it should

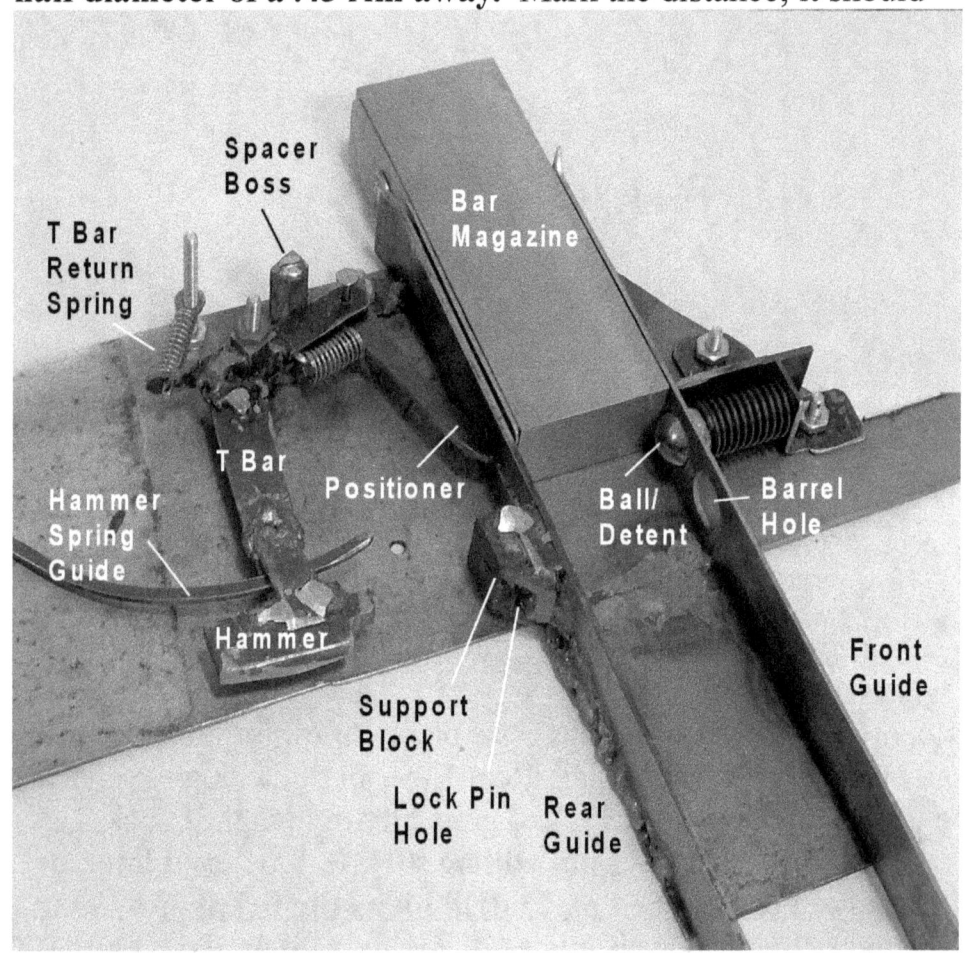

Fig. 30. View of Assembly

be about (0.24 + 0.0625) inches below the center location position of the cartridge. The Lock Pin will be described in Chapter 9.

The Firing Pin

The firing pin assembly is a minor build, simply a small steel block with the firing pin itself embedded into the block. See Figure 31. The heavy hammer will impact the firing pin to fire a cartridge, and a spring from the Ace Spring Assortment 5213517 will be used as a return spring. A small step at the top can be used with a stop to retain the firing pin in the receiver and rear magazine guide. It is to limit the firing pin from falling out of the receiver.

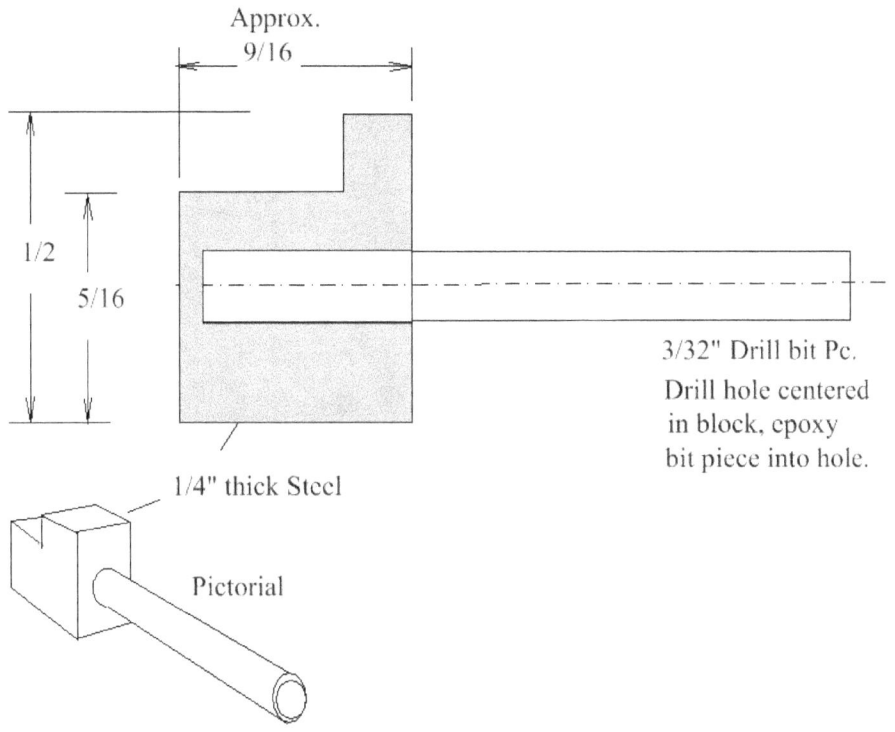

Fig. 31. Firing Pin Assembly

Or you can drill a side hole and epoxy in a side pin as a stop. I actually did the latter, six of one, half dozen of the other... either way is fine. **However, during test firing in Chapter 12, the**

pin fell out and I had to redo it... When I redid it, I welded on a small nib which made it equivalent to Figure 31.

Make a small "L" bracket with a tab to act as a guide for the firing pin as well as a stop to prevent the firing pin from falling from the receiver. See Figure 32. Make sure the stop tab does not interfere with the hammer, make a modification if needed, narrowing the stop tab. You could also make another guide bracket similar, except without the stop. This would provide an upper and lower guide on either side of the firing pin. In my version, I did not make a second guide, the drill bit pin was very strong.

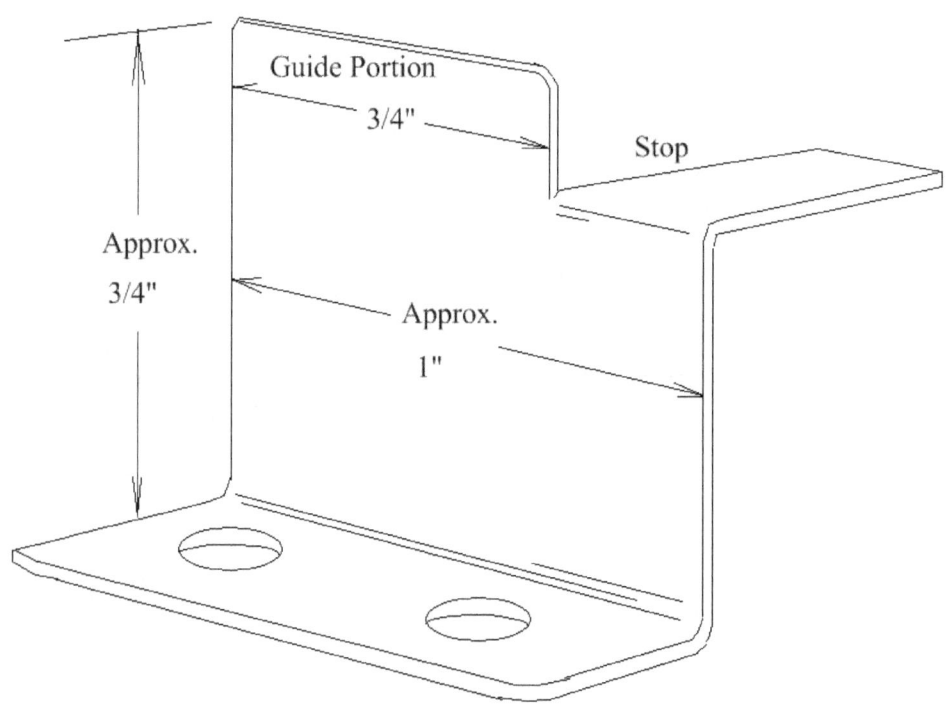

Fig. 32. Firing Pin Guide

You will probably need to shorten the firing pin so that when pushed in, it will just protrude enough to fire a cartridge when the Positioner is at the top of the rear magazine guide slot. If too long, with a round in position, the pin will restrict the "T" arm and Positioner from returning high in the slot to grab the next round above. Carefully trim it off with the Dremel Tool cutoff disk, then use the Dremel Tool with a small grinder tip to gently round the firing pin tip. If you use a drill bit as I did, it will be quite hard.

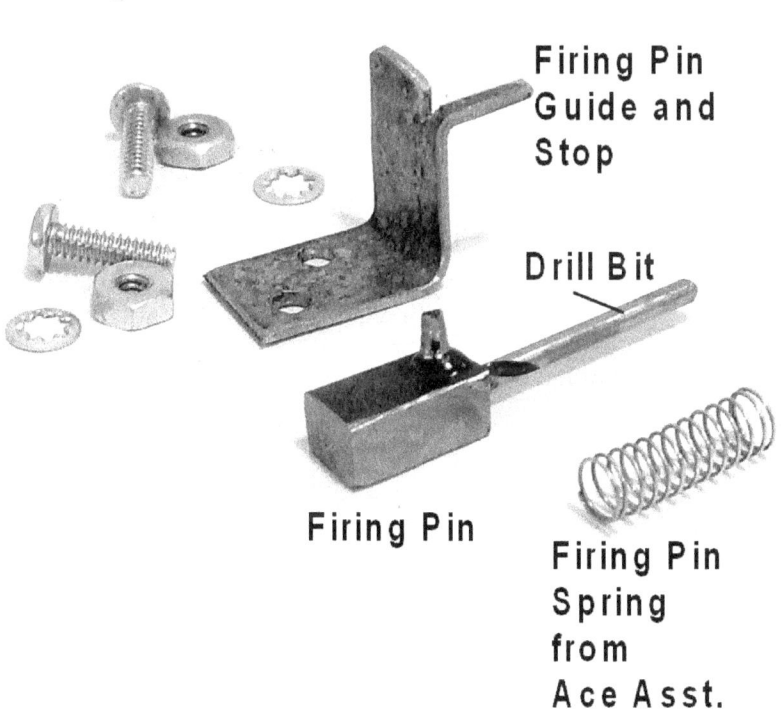

Fig. 33. Photo of Actual Firing Pin and Stop

The firing pin return spring may also need to be shortened

slightly; this will be one of the small springs from the Ace Compression Spring Assortment. However, my spring did not need shortening.

Figure 33 shows the actual parts that I made; later I did modify the firing pin to be stepped as in Figure 31.

Assembling the Hammer

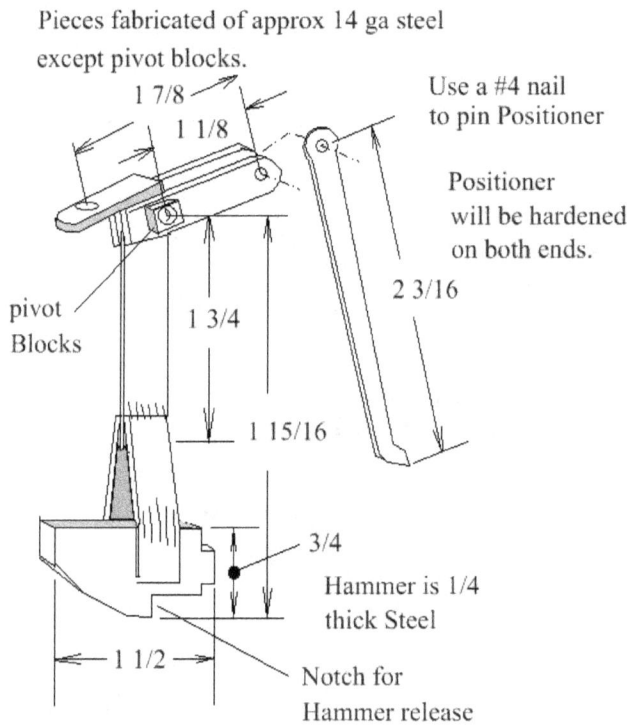

Fig. 34. Hammer Installation on "T" Bar

Next look at Figure 34, which shows the method of attaching the hammer to the "T" Bar assembly. The hammer is made from a chunk of 1/4" Steel, about 3/4" x 1 ½ " in size. A curved ramp is cut with the Angle Grinder at the rear half of the chunk. This ramp will be the portion which slides up onto the hammer release mechanism.

Then cut a 3/16" notch out as shown in the drawing. This is the hammer catch notch, which catches and holds the hammer at the cocked position. You will also note a step built onto the front of the hammer as well; this can be done later to center the strike point on the firing pin block. Final dimensions for my build are shown in Figure 34.

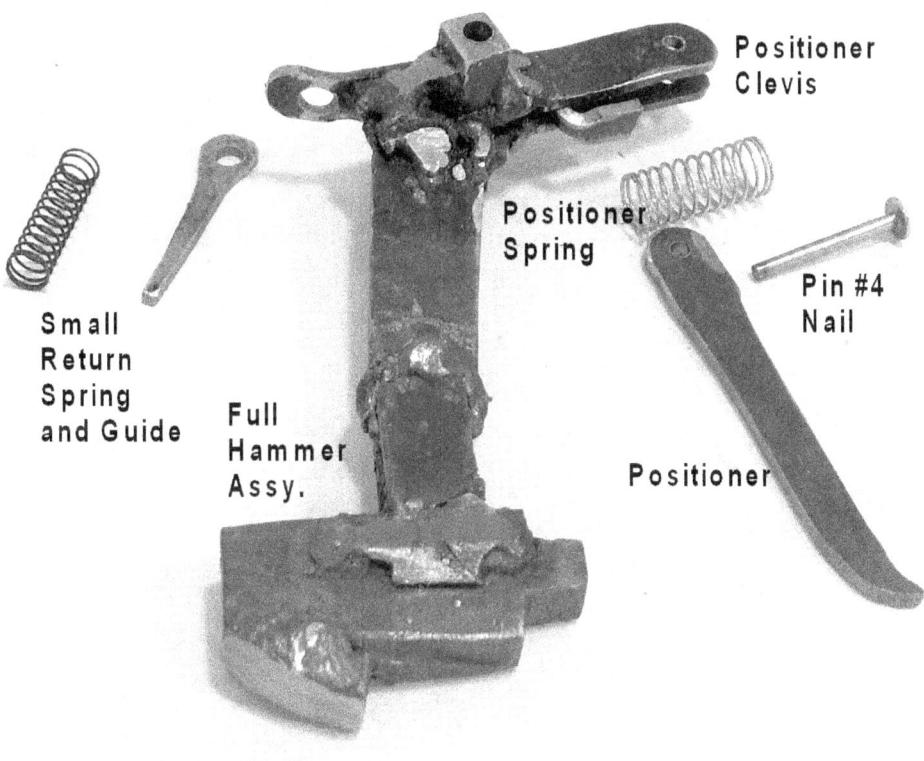

Fig. 35. Entire Hammer Assembly and Parts

Two thin straps are welded to each side of the 1/4" thick

hammer block and are bent in to pinch onto the lower "T" arm. It may be necessary to remove a bit of the lower "T" arm for later mounting of the hammer to the arm, making sure of the hammer and firing pin alignment with the arm pivoting in the receiver panel.

As discussed earlier, it is a good idea to weld a reinforcing rib onto the front of the lower "T" arm... this is needed as the hammer spring is strong and will twist the assembly during cocking otherwise. I did not do this until test firing in Chapter 12 when the weakness became apparent.

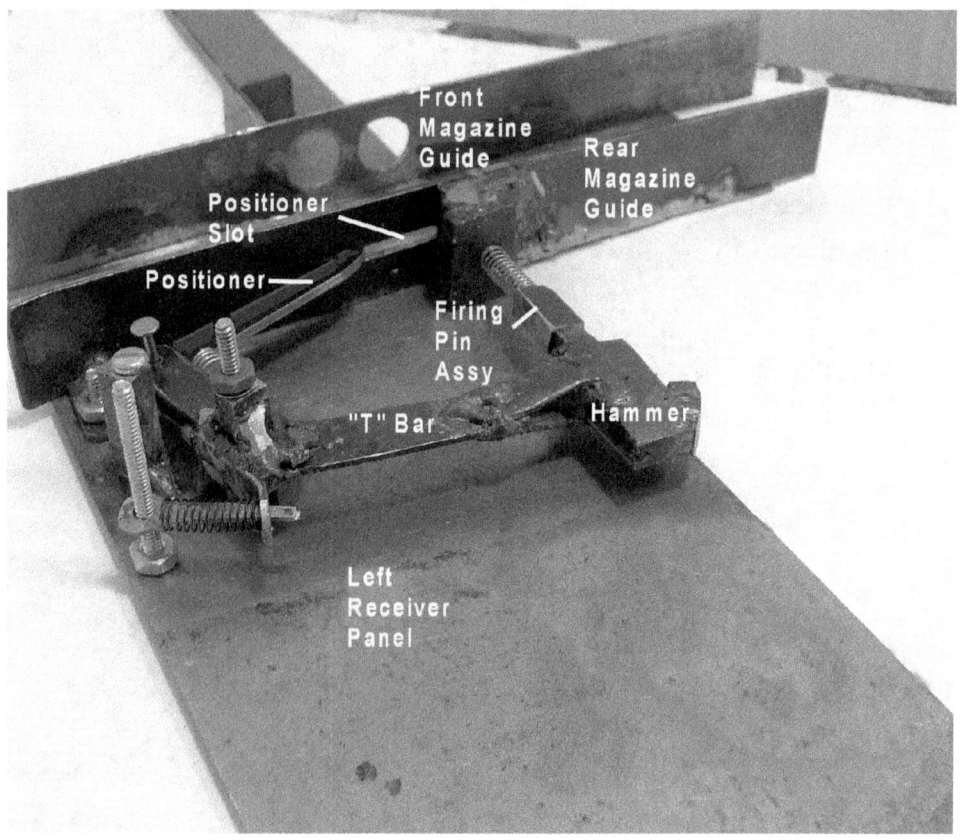

Fig. 36. Hammer and Firing Pin View

You will not see this in the photos until Chapter 12 as I added it after the test firing.

After placing the firing pin in place, a careful check can be made for hammer setup onto the lower "T" arm so the hammer will be horizontal where it aligns with the firing pin block. A straight, in-line strike is desired. Once the position is determined, remove the "T" assembly and weld the hammer onto the lower arm. Clean off weld splatter and beads. Figure 35 shows the finished unit.

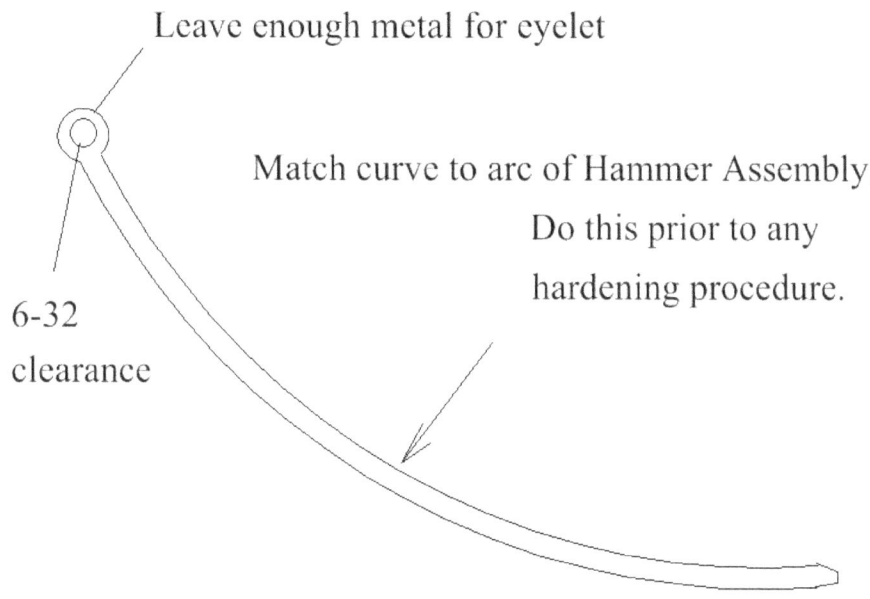

Fig. 37. Hammer Spring Guide

Now see Figure 36, which shows setup thus far of the hammer and firing pin addition.

Next build a spring guide for the hammer assembly. This is nothing more than a long thin Steel piece, which will fit inside the hammer spring thus keeping any springs in alignment. It should be made long and should have an enlarged loop at one end for the lock pin. Any extra length can be cut off later.

Bend the guide into a fairly accurate arc to match the arc of the "T" Bar and hammer assembly. See Figure 37.

Check to verify and also locate a point near the upper part of the receiver panel to attach the pinned end. In my build, this turned out about 7/8" from the top of the receiver and about 4 1/2" back from the rear guide. Use a 6-32 screw for this mounting, and keep in mind the guide should be positioned about halfway between the receiver sides once finalized. You may add some spacer to center the guide between the receiver panels.

Take pains to insure the hammer will not hit the firing pin guide and stop piece.

The final configuration at this stage is shown in Figure 38. I did temporarily stick a hammer spring on for the photo, also note the firing pin guide is shown installed.

I have one more comment, which is very important:
It is very desirable to have the hammer remain in contact with the firing pin through the motion into the magazine area and contact with a round... ***this is due to the additional mass and energy being imparted to to the firing pin as it strikes the primer.*** Without that additional mass momentum, the light firing pin would strike with less force on the round. So make sure the forward tab on the hammer is sufficient. (or later you can weld a bump on the front portion if needed...)

Finally, weld a 1 1/2" length of 1/4" steel rod perpendicular to the side surface of the hammer as a hammer handle for cocking.

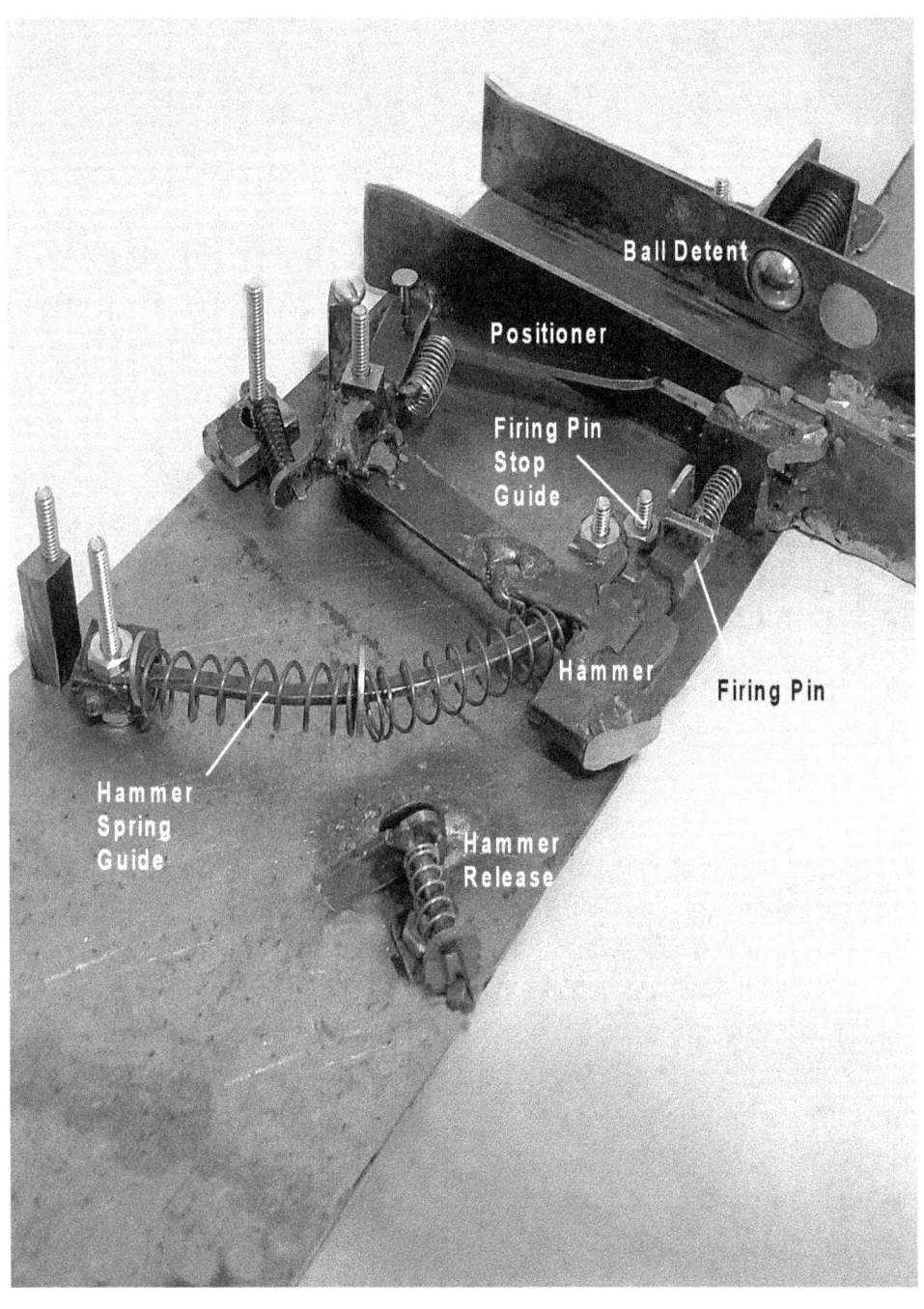

Fig. 38. Build with Hammer Spring Guide

------------------------------**NOTE:** ------------------------------

Do NOT use any live rounds from this point on as you test the Positioner and operation, make sure you have spent rounds in the Bar Magazine.

DANGER!!

Do NOT put a hammer spring in your configuration. From this point on the rifle assembly could fire with a real spring installed!!!!!!

*********SPECIAL NOTE:** *******

Sometimes while doing some of the build portion of the gun in this more detailed and complicated phase, my own fabrication was not exactly as described. I had many metal parts and pieces left over from the previous .22 rifle, and tried to use any metal pieces that adapted. Many small pieces of Steel were about the right size for brackets, etc.

But my intent in the drawings and instructions is to simplify or incorporate an entirely adequate or improved version that might possibly differ a bit from my photos. Please realized this as you work on the parts, many workable variations exist for any part, and I tried to improve the design as it was built. A part may look different, but it can still function just fine. Your ideas may be an ideal way, also.

Chapter 7

Hammer Release
and Trigger

From this point forward, a builder must be very careful to attach parts in a way to allow removal for repair, assembly, etc. … do NOT weld any part in a way to impede removal or later assembly as you finish the build. I speak from experience here!

And NO LIVE ROUNDS!!

Hammer Release

At this point it is time to do the hammer release and design the trigger setup. The hammer release is made up of two "L" brackets and a bit of #16 nail, which when combined with a spring will form a simple release mechanism.

See Figure 39 on the next page for the design. Cut two piece of the 14 gauge sheet Steel, approximately 1/2" wide and about 2" long, and bend into two "L" brackets; one arm will be ½ to 5/8" long as the base, the other will be the taller vertical portion guiding the release rod.

Use a punch on the upright portions of the "L" brackets and mark a centered spot for drilling a 9/64" hole about 7/16" from the base, this will be about ½ the distance between receiver panels for aligning with a centered hammer assembly.

The rod is made next from a length of smooth 16 penny nail. Use the Dremel tool and cutoff disk to remove the head, leaving a clean shaft.

About 1/2" from one end, clamp the nail in a bench vise and tap the nail over to form a 90 degree bend in the nail. This will form the portion that is grabbed by the trigger when the rifle is fired.

Figure 39 shows the construction and Figure 40 shows the actual piece on the next page.

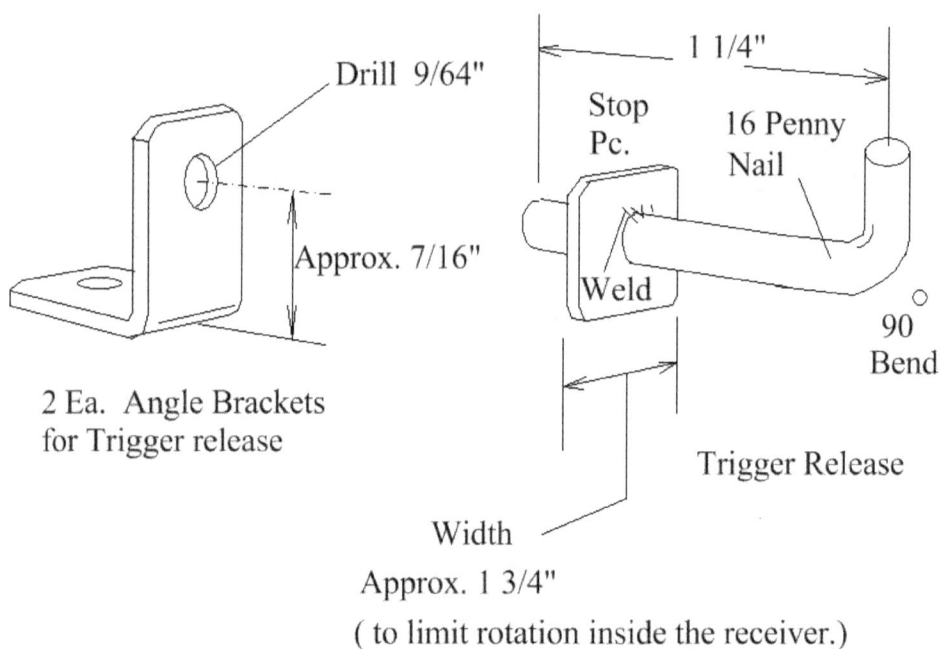

Fig. 39. Details For Hammer Release Mechanism

A small stop piece is welded about 1/4" from the non bent end to set the movement range. This piece should be long enough to prevent the nail portion from rotating once installed in the receiver. A suitable spring can be slid over the bent portion of the nail, following with the bracket placed over the end. This welding is tricky with such small parts, and you do not want to allow too long a heat interval, a simple tack of the stop is all that is necessary here.

Fig. 40. Hammer Release Rod

Once this part is made it can be placed on the receiver panel to determine the final location in relation to the other parts. Place the assembly so it will retain the hammer at the full cock position with the Positioner bottomed out at the bottom of the slot in the rear guide. It should end up in a position such that the hammer release rod is aligned radially to the "T" bar rotation and pivot point. The upper angle bracket can be welded to the receiver once the correct position is located, the lower bracket should be mounted with a screw, lock washer and nut to allow replacement or repair if ever required. See Figure 41.

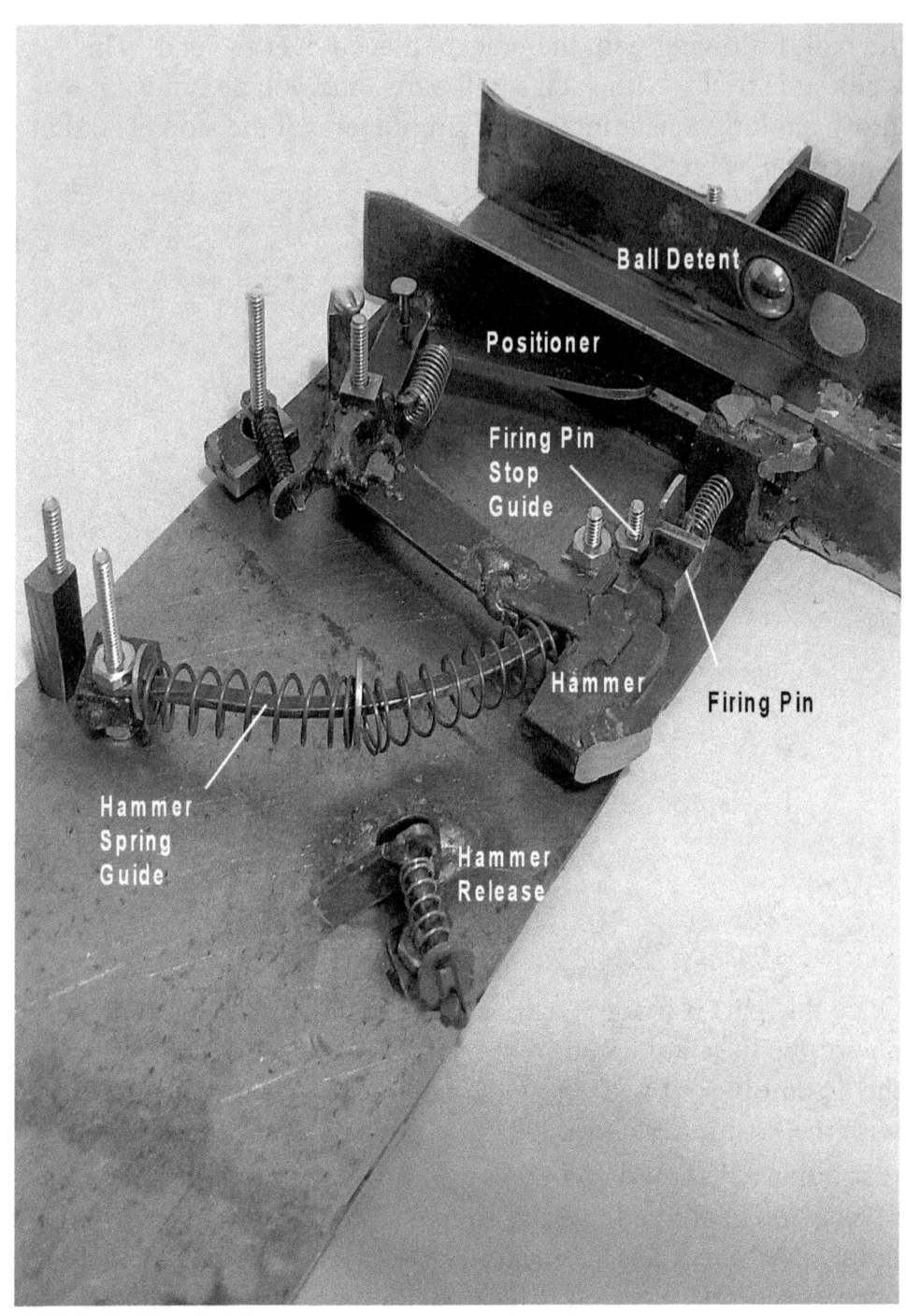

Fig. 41. Hammer Release

CAUTION !!!

From this point on, use only fired .45 cartridges in the Bar Magazine in any testing! As we install more and more parts the rifle is approaching the capability of firing a cartridge!

Trigger Assembly

Back when I did "Homebuilt Firearms", I had actually made two trigger pieces. The pieces are rough cut using the Angle Grinder, then final work is done with a round file and Dremel Tool, even carbide sandpaper possibly. I will use that trigger with any modification required for the .45 Carbine to save time.

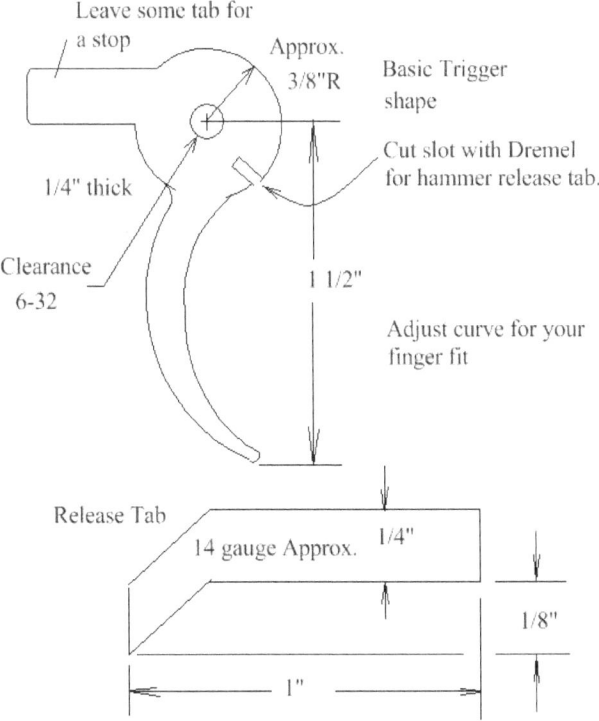

Fig. 42. General Trigger Assembly

The trigger piece should be cut from a scrap of 1/4" Steel using the Angle Grinder with a cutoff disk. Cut it out roughly, then use the bench grinder to get closer. Once you have gotten it roughly shaped finish the job with a round file and Dremel Tool.

You can use a tiny drum sander on the Dremel to do a nice smooth job as you round the front of the trigger to get it comfortable for your finger. Once you have it nicely shaped, use the Dremel with a cutoff disk to cut a slot in the lower front quarter of the trigger as shown in Figure 42.

Set the trigger roughly into place on the receiver assembly. Visualize the hammer release tab at the location and also remember the trigger should be centered between the receiver sides.

With the centering in mind, stack a few pieces of Steel beneath the trigger as it sits in place to adjust it approximately to center above the assembled receiver. You will see as you position the piece that the hammer release stub must be further from the receiver panel than the trigger, this is why it is made as shown in Figure 42. Poke it into the slot in the trigger and check how you must weld it for proper functioning. Then carefully remove the trigger and stub, clamp them accordingly and weld the release stub onto the trigger assembly; a fairly minimal spot weld will suffice.

Replace the new trigger assembly onto the receiver and align it with the stacked spacing again to get the approximate height from the panel.

The release tab should essentially ride just above the hammer release and you can carefully bend the tab to sort of "hook" loosely over the bent end.

Determine the proper pivot point for the trigger... on my rifle this came out 3/8" from the bottom of the receiver and about 5 1/2" back from the rear guide.

It is acceptable to bend the release stub as needed to set up a nice operation. Redo if you have to but once you are happy with the trigger setup, make a small angle piece to form a trigger stop. Mount it so that it will block the trigger stop just as the hammer releases from the release point on the hammer/ "T" Bar unit.

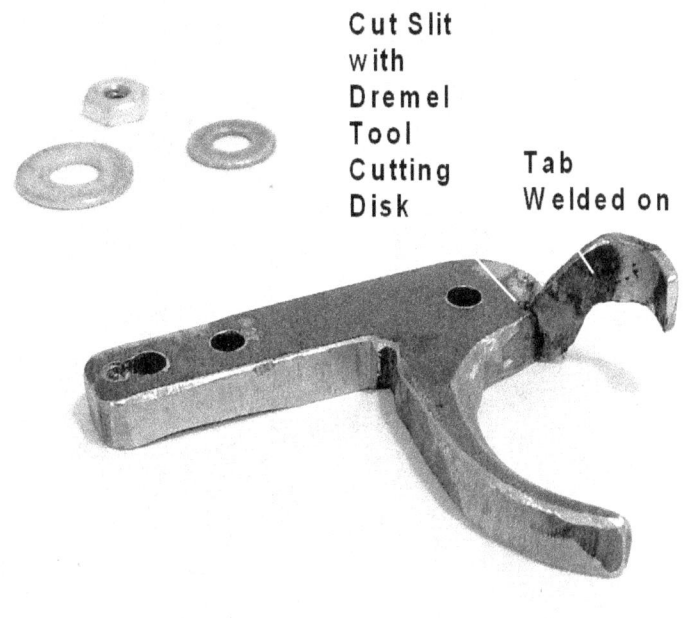

Fig. 43. Actual Trigger Assembly

See Figure 43 for my actual trigger and Figure 44 for the assembly. Note the release tab is bent slightly to hook the hammer release rod. And it sits higher than the trigger level. Look at Figure 44 on the next page. This shows the parts mounting to this point. This a view from the "top" of the receiver. A bit odd, but it shows the firing pin guide/ stop clearly and a fairly good view of the hammer release and trigger. Figure 45 on the following page is another view.

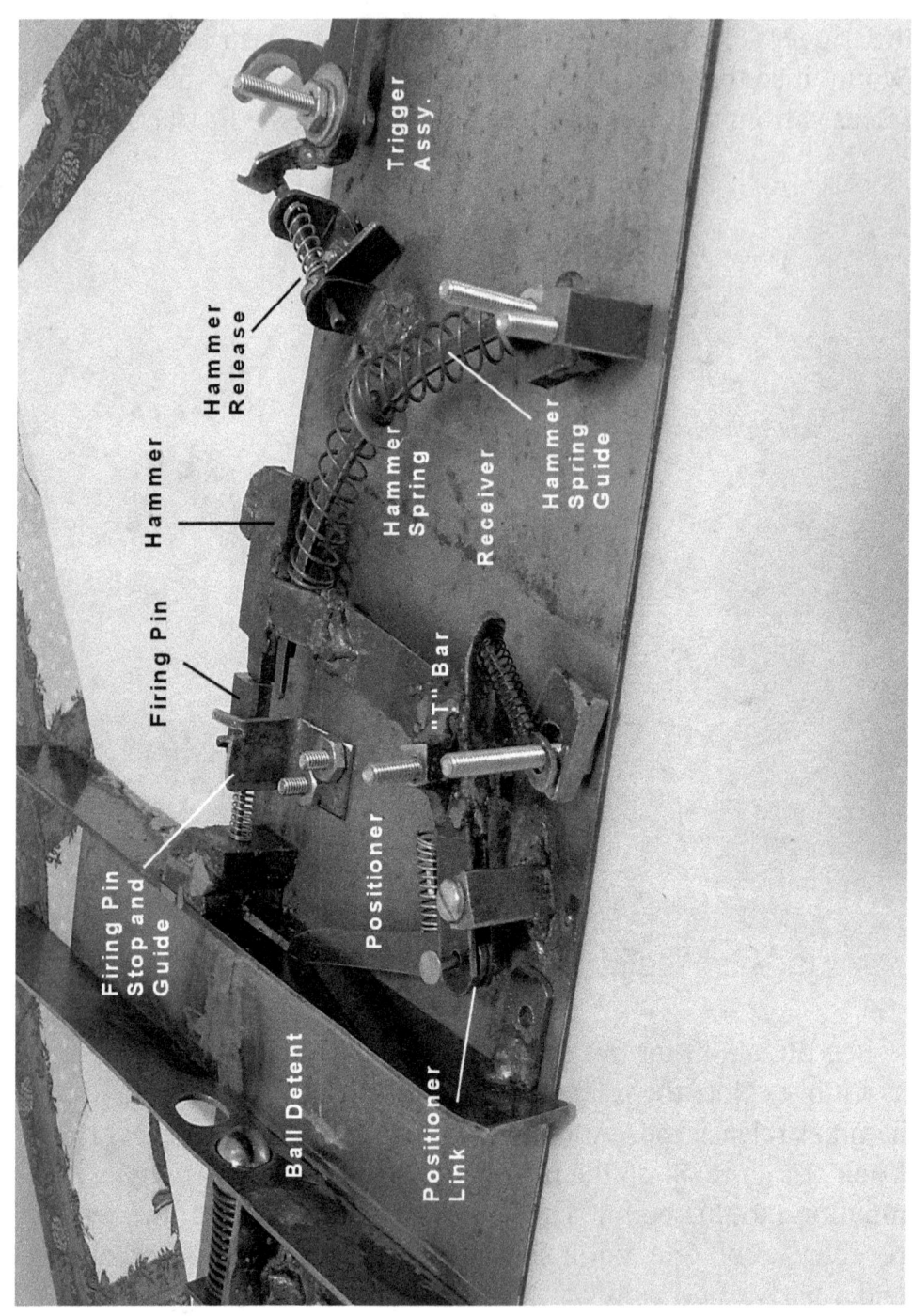

Fig. 44. View From Top

Fig. 45. Most Parts Installed

Chapter 8

Hardening of Critical Parts

Some of the Steel parts in the gun are subject to continued abrasion and rubbing, also the firing pin must be hardened to avoid mushrooming. It turns out this is not a difficult process. Read up a bit on the internet to study the basic principle.

The Hardening Process

Because all these parts are small, this is a fairly easy job. It requires heating a part --or portion of a part-- Red Hot using a propane type torch, (Except use MAPP gas which is much hotter...) then immediately dropping the part into oil. Used motor oil is my choice, it probably has additional carbon content over clean oil. Also I found the part that was hardened took on a black appearance and made it easy to tell what area had been hardened. The part essentially absorbs carbon from the oil into the surface, which hardens it on the surface. With the small parts we are working with, it only takes a few seconds to heat a part red hot.

You should have the oil in a small shallow can, like a Tuna Fish can, and also work clear of anything flammable. Have a flat metal cover to place over the oil can in case of any flames.

This process also makes the part brittle though, so a second process is used to relieve stresses in the steel. The part is placed in an oven at about 400 degrees for an hour or so, which allows the stresses to relax or relieve from the metal.

The final product will be tough and have a very hard surface for abrasion resistance. It will seem more "slippery" in rubbing against other parts, the change is pretty amazing. For example,

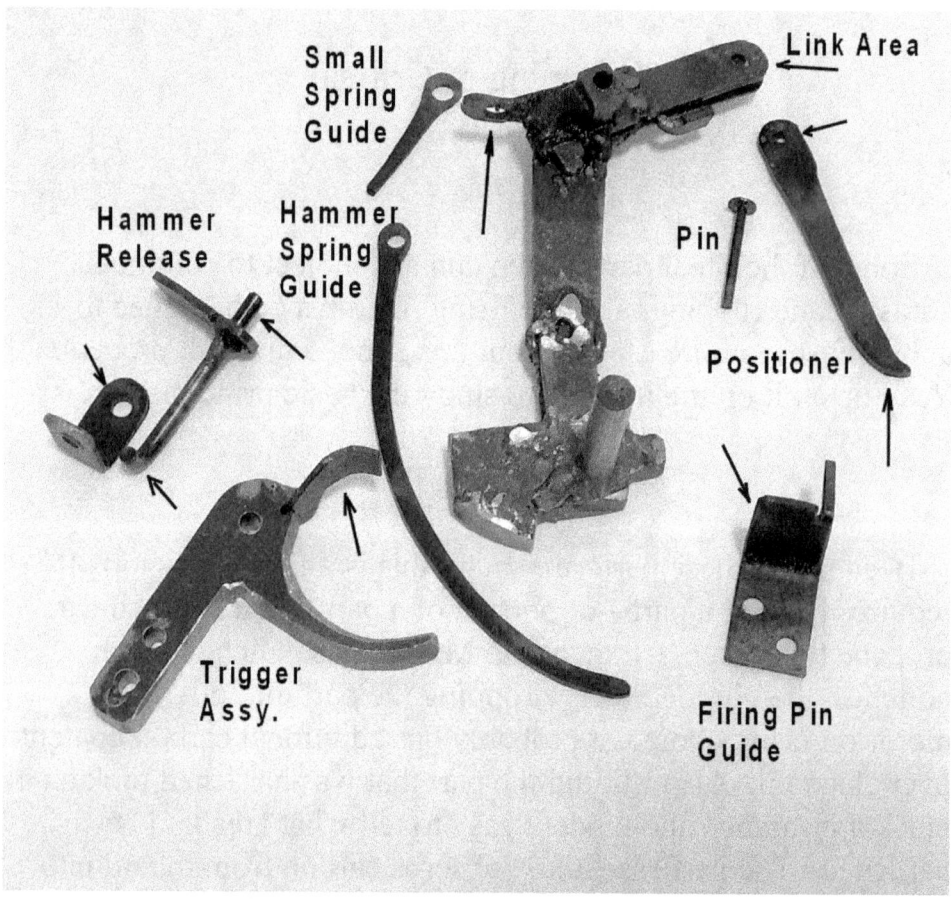

Fig. 46. Small Receiver Parts

the Hammer Spring Guide will seem a lot more "slippery" when operating with a spring. Look at the parts shown in Figure 46. Of the parts shown, both ends of the Positioner should be hardened, the Hammer Spring Guide should be hardened along its length <u>after it is shaped</u>, and the ends of the Hammer Release Rod (nail) and the upper "L" bracket should be done.

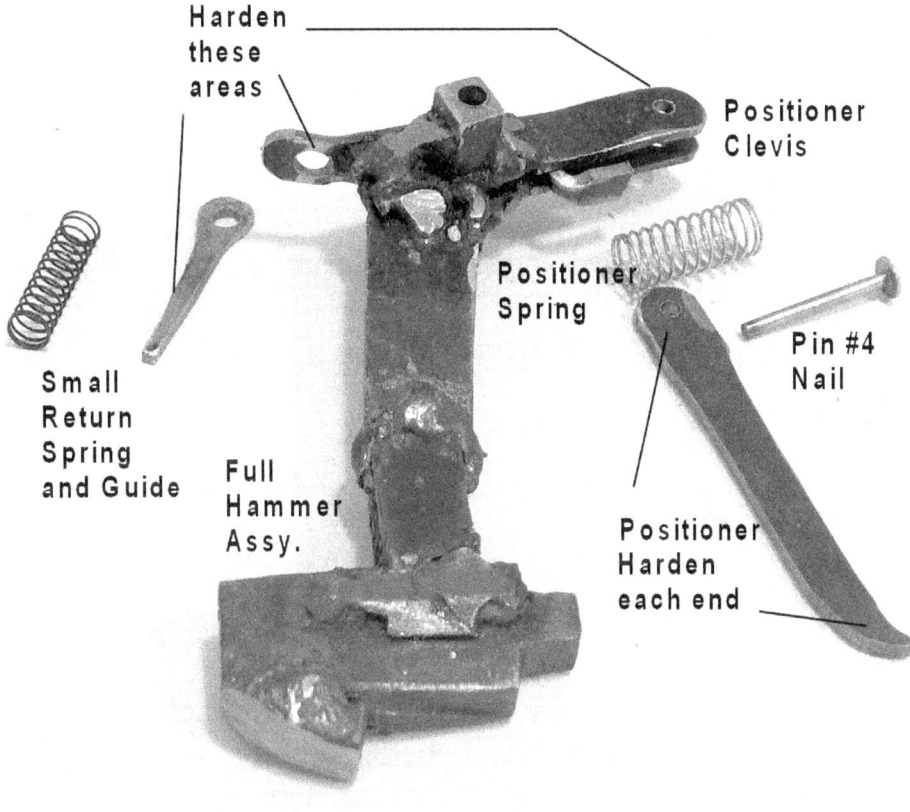

Fig. 47. Areas to Harden on "T" Bar

In addition, I believe the upper link and return spring portion of the "T" Bar should be hardened and the rim locking mechanism tip described in the next chapter, which catches the rim of the cartridges as they ratchet down through the gun. Probably no need for other areas – these are the more critical parts.

When working on a part, be especially careful...

- Have a fire extinguisher handy and do not work near any flammable materials, oil or gasoline cans, etc.

- wear your safety goggles or face shield.

- Use vise-grip pliers to safely hold parts as you heat them.

- Be very careful with the MAPP gas and torch... <u>stay clear of flammables.</u>

- Before handling any parts be careful they are cooled, or use protection.

- Keep a cover handy to cover the oil can.

Use the propane Torch with MAPP gas to heat each area to red hot, than drop it immediately into the oil. Used motor oil should be excellent, having even more carbon content. You can repeat the process twice perhaps and maybe obtain a deeper hardening process.

The Tempering Process

Once you have done the oil hardening process, and the parts are cooled, wipe them clean, perhaps wash off with some alcohol or paint thinner. After totally dry, place them on a small throw-away pie pan and into an oven. Adjust the heat to about 375 to 400 degrees, and let them remain in the oven for about 1 ½ hours. After the time interval has passed, turn off the oven, and let the parts cool in the oven, later on use a hot pad and remove them from the oven.

After the parts are fully cooled you may oil them a bit and set aside for assembly.

NOTE:

Some of the parts in the next chapter should also be hardened and tempered, specifically the Chamber Lock Device. You should jump ahead and make it prior to doing the process. No need to fire up the oven for only one small item, do them all at once.

Chapter 9

Finishing the Receiver

REMEMBER: NO LIVE ROUNDS while testing the mechanism !!

There are only a few items remaining with the receiver, but they are important. Once in a great while, the Positioner would jump out of its guide slot during testing as it returned to the top of the rear guide. With the receiver laying flat, this allowed the Positioner to fall alongside the slot and not regain the correct position. Although this is unlikely to happen under normal upright conditions, it should be made impossible.

This is an easy fix, by merely adding a guide piece on each side... if it hops out of the slot it will simply slip right back in. I made an "L" bracket for the one receiver panel... (the bottom panel during fabrication...) with a height matched to the left side of the rear magazine guide slot. This kept it from falling out the left side of the slot.

Then I welded a small prong onto the rear magazine guide to prevent the Positioner from falling out the right side of the slot. The two guides restrict the Positioner to its sideways correct position at all times... it will not fall from the slot. See Figure 48 on the next page.

There are four other items to add in this chapter:

- Some support boss spacers to allow joining the receiver panels together at the correct spacing,

- Additional rear guide support behind the chamber area.

- The special lock pin to augment the ball detent for a solid lock for each chamber position.

- The arced slot must be cut in the right receiver panel to allow cocking the rifle.

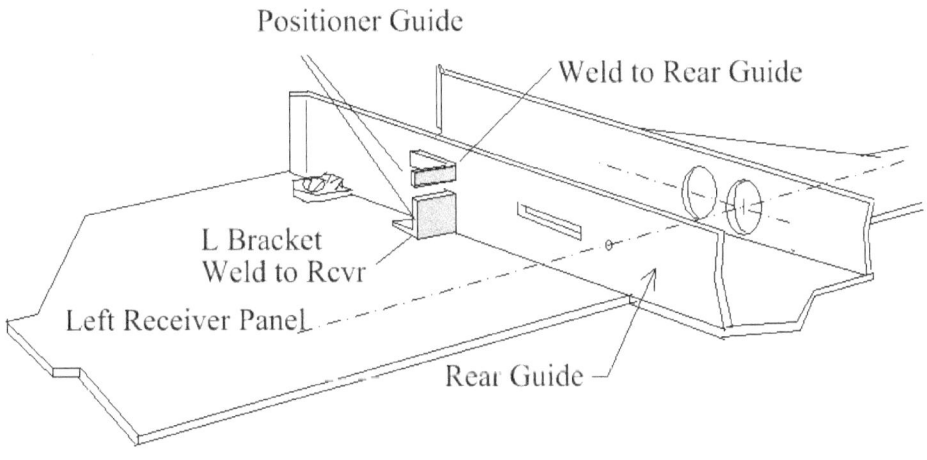

Fig. 48. Positioner Guides

Receiver Panel Spacers

   Drill three or four 6-32 clearance holes edgewise through a 1" wide piece of 1/4" Steel. The holes should be spaced about 1/2" or 5/8" apart. Then use the Angle Grinder to cut the portion into spacers, each piece of about 3/8" width. Grind them to the exact height of the front and rear Bar Magazine guides... about 0.9" high. You can drill the one receiver panel to place a spacer at similar spots to those shown in Figure 49 top and

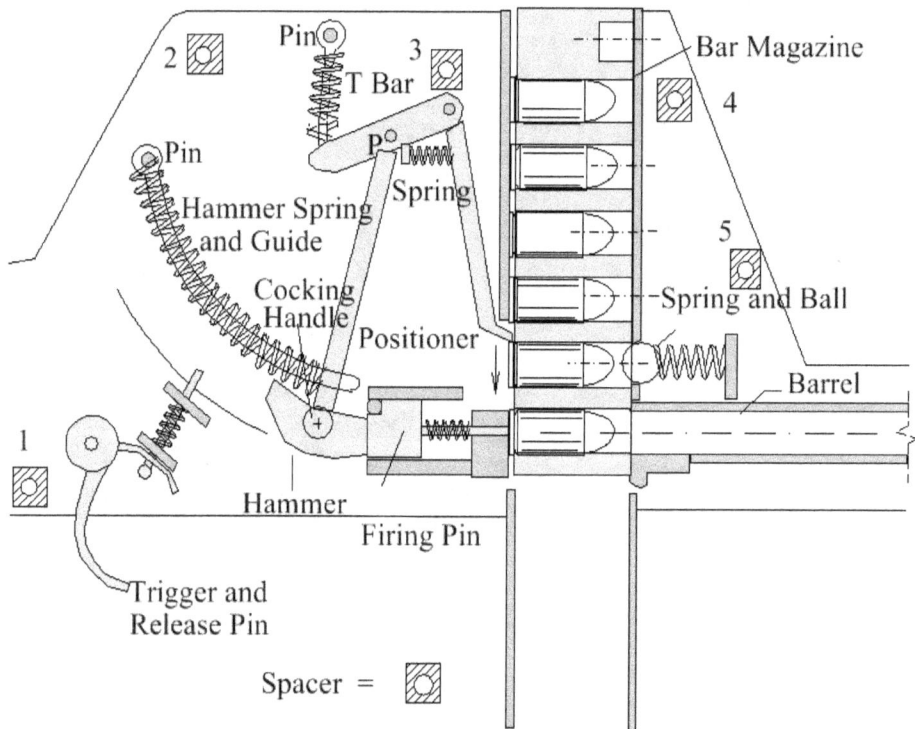

Fig. 49. Suggested Spacer Spots

bottom. I assumed about five total perhaps counting boss 3, which was already mounted back a couple of chapters as a stop for the "T" Bar. Spacer 5 is really optional as there may not be room for it ... also the barrel mounting will secure and finalize this portion of construction.

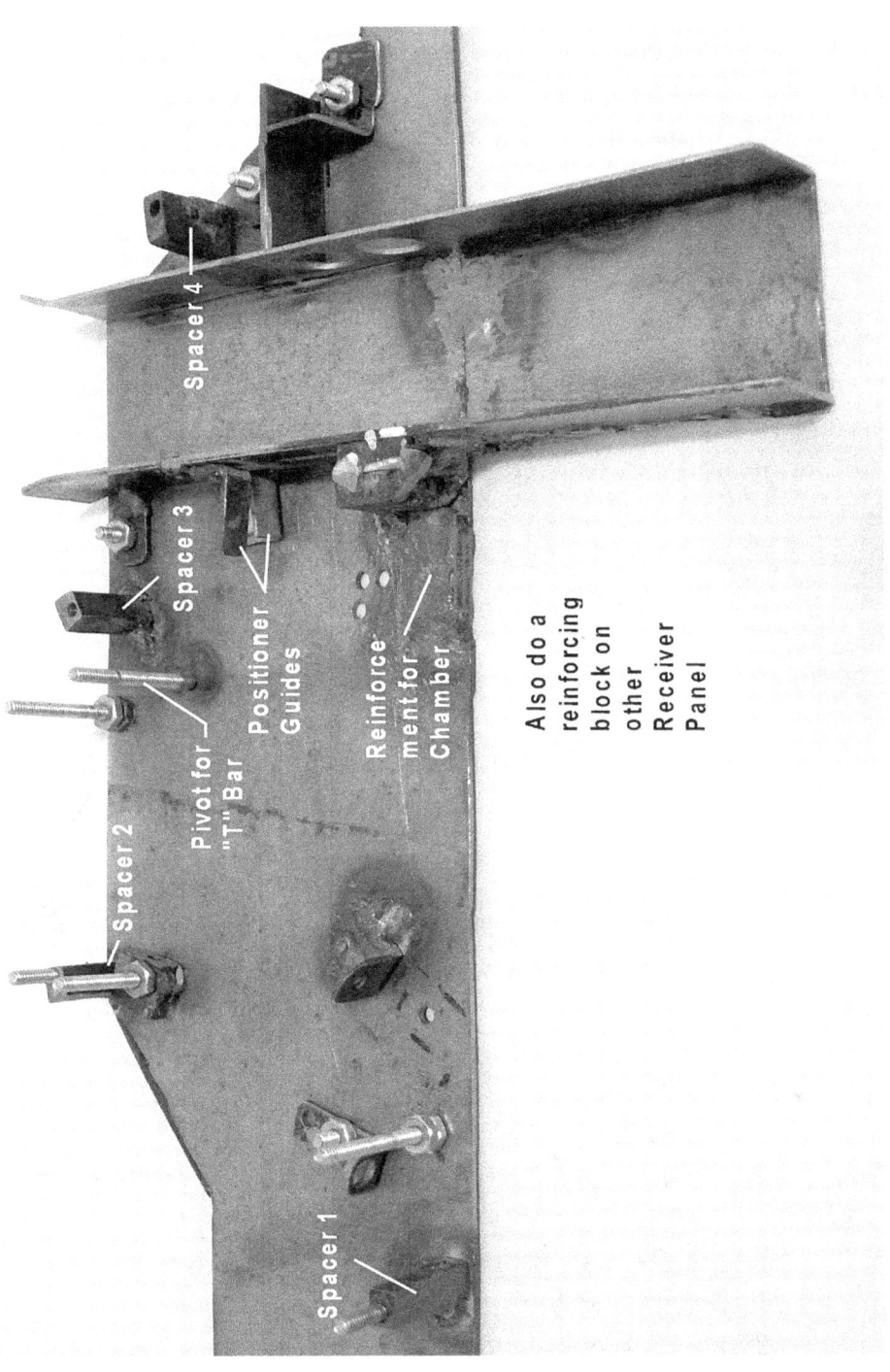

Fig. 50. View of Spacers Welded on

As the lower portion of the magazine guides are covered, additional support can be provided on the lower edge of the receiver if needed or desired.

Use a long 6-32 screw and nut to mount each spacer boss onto the one receiver panel. The spacers should stand vertically on the panel as it lays flat. Next you will tack weld each onto the panel.

As you prepare to weld the spacer pieces onto the one receiver panel, remove any parts which could be damaged, and cover the area carefully to protect the rest of the panel surface. A piece of Aluminum foil can be used as long as you place it so you won't directly hit it with your welding tip. Once you have the remaining spacer bosses welded on, clean off any spatter or debris. Use the drilled panel bosses as a guide to drill the matching holes in the other receiver panel. Check alignment as you go and finish the receiver panels so they can be joined.

Additional Support of the Rear Guide Chamber Area

The instantaneous pressure of the .45 cartridge firing is absorbed at the rear by the rear magazine guide. With 21,000 P.S.I. pressures involved, we must make certain the rear support is adequate to resist this. The rear rim area of the round is

$A = 3.14 \times (0.480/2) \times (0.480/2)$ inches $= 0.181$ sq. in.

So the force is $P \times A = 21,000 \times 0.181$ lbs $= 3800$ lbs. Max

on the metal at the rear, probably somewhat less due to the bullet immediately exiting at the front of the chamber.

Now, the metal block welded to the rear guide behind the round chamber is very rigid and strong, but the rear guide itself could flex without some brace support. So that is what I am concerned with, welding a brace on each receiver panel to back up the rear magazine guide. I had several 3/16" or so scraps of Steel, and simply cut two small strips to weld onto the receiver panels blocking right against the rear of the guide. Take care to place them so they do not interfere with the firing pin or firing pin guide. The next photo shows the receivers spacers I installed and also the block reinforcing behind the firing pin. Also do the reinforcing for the other receiver panel too, clamp it in place after carefully determining its position.

These brace pieces must rest against the existing support. Do not shim, if a space exists weld and grind to a contact fit. These braces are shown in Figure 50 and 51.

Cutting the Cocking Slot in the Right Receiver Panel

With the left receiver flat with parts mounted, Take a careful measure of the hammer handle distance from the bottom of the receiver and back from the rear magazine guide. Drill a matching hole in the right receiver panel; probably a 3/8" hole will do.

Check the position as you place the right receiver over the other, aligning your spacing bosses. File as needed for clearance of the hammer handle. Using the "T" bracket/hammer pivot holes as a center, mark the arc onto the right receiver panel for hammer rotation, for an approximate arc of 2 1/2". You can increase this later if needed.

To cut the arc, first drill a spaced series of 3/8" holes along the arc. Then, using the Dremel Tool and cutting disk, cut out between the holes to open the entire arc. Use a round file to finish into a smooth arc for hammer rotation. Check clearance as you rotate the hammer and remove any burrs on the panel.

Your panel should appear similar to Figure 51. Note the braces for the rear guide chamber area.

Fig. 51. Hammer Slot and Chamber Braces

The Chamber lock Device

Back in Chapter 5 and 6 the need for a special chamber locking pin was described briefly and a hole was drilled for this in the add on support block welded to the rear magazine guide (Chapter 6) just below the firing pin hole. Visualize what this device is meant to do:

- As the cocking motion begins with the hammer, the locking pin must move backwards to release the Bar Magazine to slide down for the next round.

- It needs to only move a fraction to clear the .45 rim to accomplish the release. This must occur just before the Bar Magazine is going to move.

- The Positioner has a tiny bit of slop before it moves down grabbing the upper portion of the next round; so there is a bit of allowable hammer movement prior to the Bar Magazine beginning its motion.

- Because the lever arm on the hammer is over twice as long as the distance from the "T" Bar pivot to the Positioner pin, the hammer movement is over twice as far as the Positioner movement... this allows the setup of the chamber lock to be fairly accurate.

- In other words, this movement should be enough to actuate the unlock of the locking pin just before the Bar Magazine begins to move. In fact it may have begun release on hammer bounce.

- On the next cocking motion, the lock pin should pull back and release the .45 rim for enough time for the Bar

Magazine to begin its lowering motion, and should not spring back until it can ride upon the rear surface of the just fired round under slight spring pressure.

- Now, the lock pin slides up the rear of the fired rim as the magazine slides downward.

- As the magazine drops further, the pin slips off the upper edge of the rim of the fired round... and jumps forward, now ready to stop the next fresh round moving into position.

- The ball detent grabs the next chamber, as the unfired round moves into place... an instant later, the hammer reaches cocked position, and the lock pin adds assurance to the correct seating of the new round at the barrel opening.

- This action is repeated for the remaining shots.

This describes the desired operation, so now to design the mechanism.

- The device must pull the lock pin back <u>immediately</u> as the hammer is moved;

- It must release and move forward after further hammer movement and only a tiny movement of the Bar magazine.

- It must remain in forward spring loaded position through the entire function as the next round seats and remain there until the hammer falls and fires the round.

- Then the operation repeats.

Look at the proposed design in Figure 52.

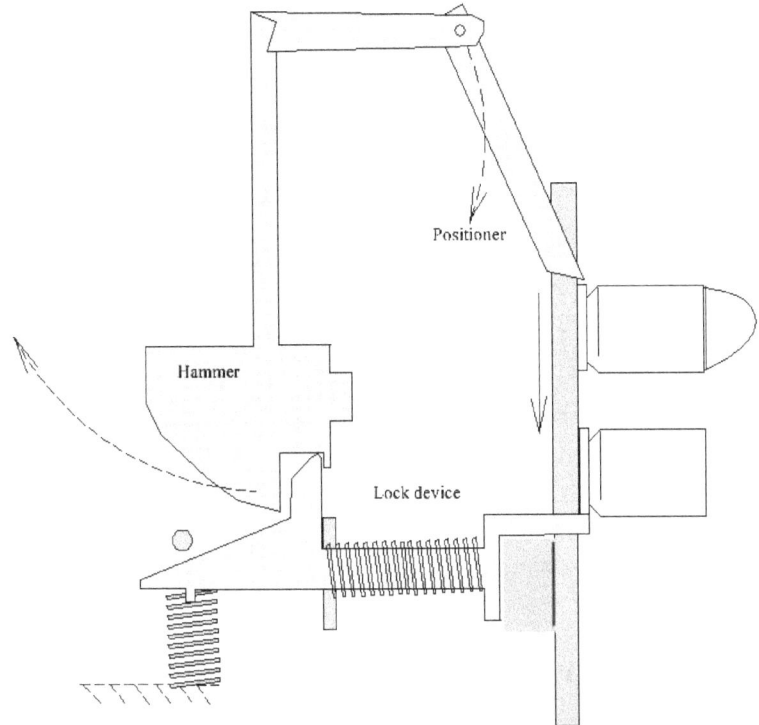

Fig. 52. Simplified Lock Pin Mechanism

This is a simplified view but gives a general idea. A little nib on the hammer grabs an angled nib on the lock mechanism, as the hammer begins rotating left in the cocking motion.

It begins pulling the lock pin assembly rearward, releasing the rim of the fired round ---however, very quickly, as the horizontal lock device assembly hits the stop pin, the hammer nib jumps free as the lock device levers downward and releases from the hammer which continues rotating... the lock device springs forward again. The stop is adjusted so this happens as the fired cartridge rim slides past. The lock device can lever a bit with careful filing and rounding of the forward pin... the movement required is very small.

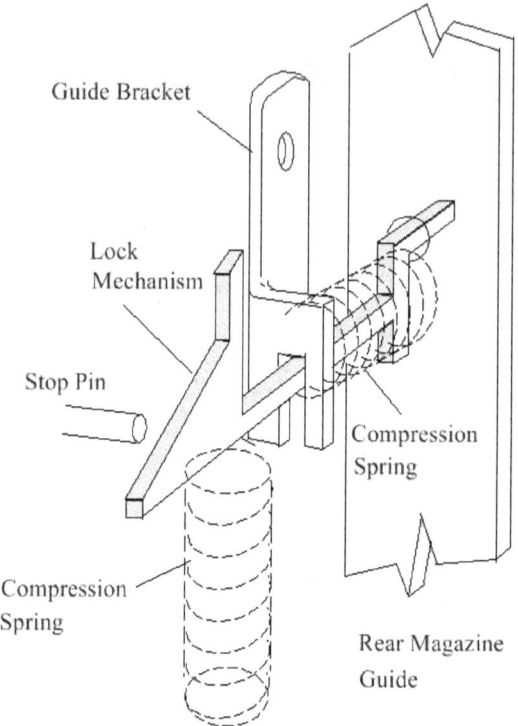

Fig. 53. View From Rear

The front portion of the lock pin mechanism now initially rides on the rear surface of the fired round as the Bar Magazine slides downward, then as it clears the upper portion of the rim, it slides forward to be set to grab the rim of the unfired round moving downward. It then provides a secure safety lock alignment with the barrel as the next chamber is grabbed by the ball detent. Any sort of grabbing device for catching the hammer may be used ... **but the general idea is the same.**

The guide slot bracket shown should be screw mounted to the left receiver to be consistent with our setup thus far.

The design is entirely workable as shown, however the geometry of the real gun dictates the actual fit and perhaps some variation. And I used a Pallet Band piece for the left spring.

Some examination of the movement required will give us some of the sizes and data needed to build the actual parts... also my build guided me into some things to remember... in looking at Figures 52 and 53 for example... it has to be possible to get the spring on the lock mechanism so obviously, there must be a way to take the piece apart to set those springs in place.

In the mechanism, remember there is a space between the Positioner and the rim of the round prior to the hammer being moved from rest. This is the designed gap to insure the Positioner is **above** the rim at rest so it can move the Bar Magazine down in the cocking cycle. Also the movement of the hammer is related to that Positioner movement by the ratio of the lower arm length to the Positioner clevis arm length. This means the hammer itself moves a greater distance than the Positioner.

Note also that the hammer movement moves the lock device exactly that same amount as it moves. It directly operates on the lock mechanism. During the vertical gap movement before the Positioner hits the rim of the next round, the hammer must begin moving the lock mechanism out of its lock position with the fired round below.

Knowing this allows us to determine the **exact point** where the lock has to move out of the way from blocking the rim of the fired round... thus allowing the Bar Magazine to ratchet down to the next chamber and cartridge.

If you carefully observe the hammer nib position just as the Positioner touches the next round, that is the point where the lock must have just cleared out of the way of the round just fired, and movement can now proceed. So, just to the right of that point... the same increment as the lock protrudes into the magazine guide, is the point where the lock mechanism catches on the hammer nib.

See Figure 54, which shows the detail. Note "d" ; this is essentially the movement required to pull the lock pin from the magazine area. Point 1 is easily picked by observing point 2 where the Positioner just touches the rim of the round above... then marking to the right the amount "d". This is where the lock must initially be grabbed by the hammer... since the hammer movement is at least twice the movement of the Positioner, these three points are very close, and best accomplished as you observe and mark your points. The lock release should occur as the rim of the fired round just passes in front of the lock pin, so the pin will slide along it and jump in to catch the next unfired round rim.

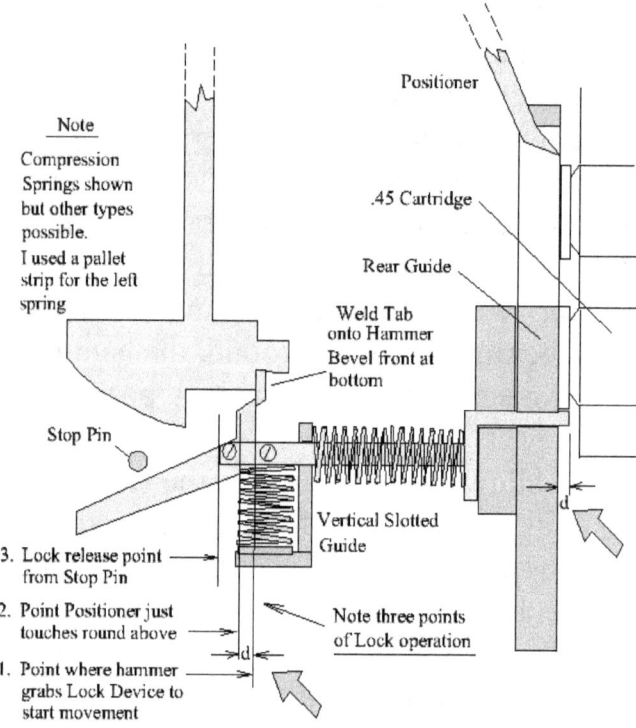

Fig. 54. Details of Lock Device

Right about point 2 the stop pin should just be starting to initiate release of the lock. This can be set as you watch and operate the lock. You can carefully grind the hammer catch nib on the lock unit to get the correct start point. This is a very critical part of the rifle, so take your time here... get it perfect.

I spent the better part of three or four days on this portion, ground a slight bit off the tip that grabs the rim, distance "d" so that it wouldn't grab the rim lock piece on the Bar Magazine, smoothing all the rubbing parts, etc.

In the cocked position, the lock pin should have the bottom of the rim, and the Positioner has the top.

Harden the Parts

Smooth all rubbing portions with fine carbide paper *in the direction of movement.* Then the parts should be hardened and tempered as described in the previous chapter, the tip that locks the cartridge rim, and sliding parts like the long portion that slides in the bracket slot, the tooth on the lock device that catches on the hammer, and the bracket slot. Also the ramp, which hits the stop pin. Figures 55 and 56 show the finalized setup to suit my rifle.

Prior to hardening, the parts were sort of grabbing and catching, but once hardened and tempered, the pieces worked flawlessly when I used nested springs for the ball detent. (See the Springs Chapter 11 …)

Dimensions are not shown, however my front portion of the lock device was about 2 5/8"L and the tip portion to grab the rim was a bit less than 7/16"L. The tip will be ground off for a perfect grab that avoids the rim lock strip but grabs the round rims.

I drilled and threaded the front portion of the device for 4-40 screws using a tap so the ramp portion could be fastened after the springs were installed.

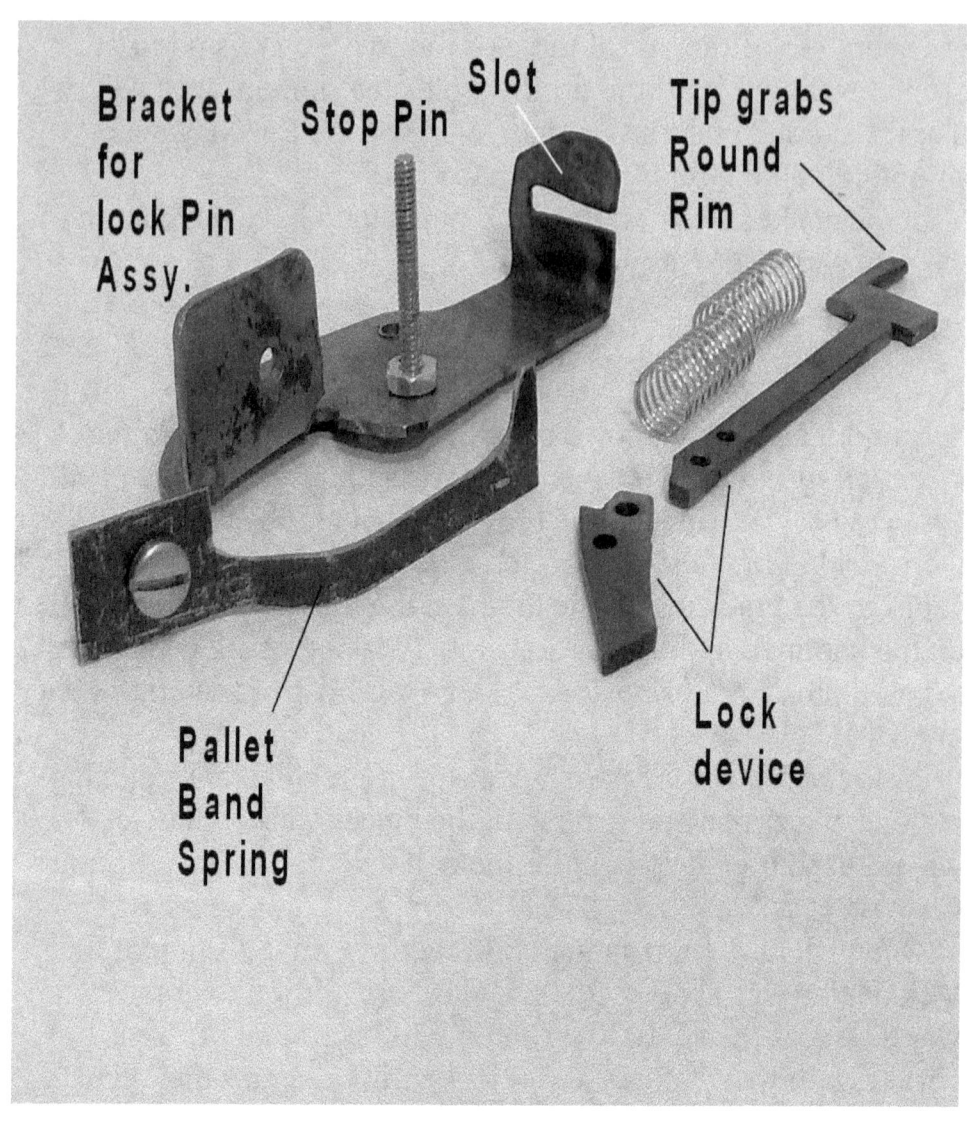

Fig. 55. Lock device Parts.

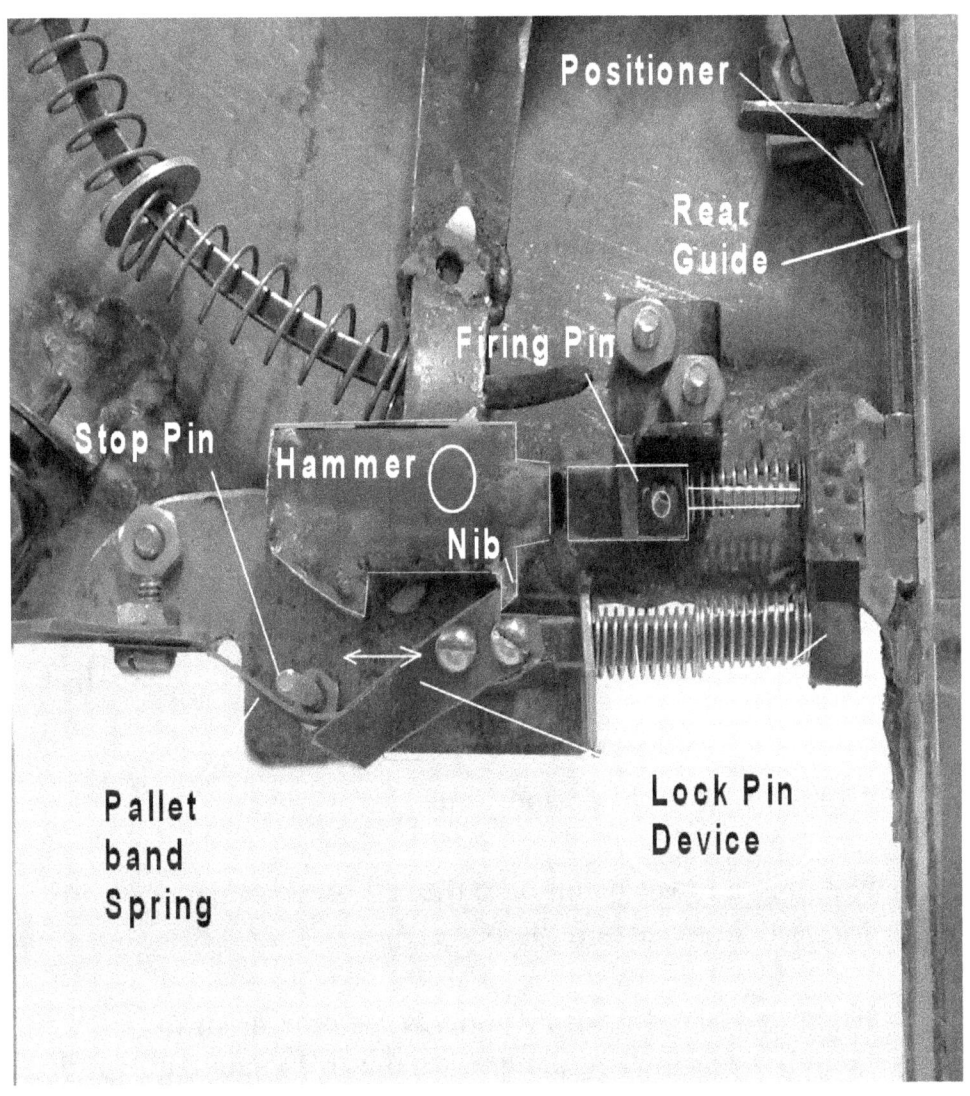

Fig. 56. Actual Lock Device Installed

Chapter 10

Fitting the Barrel

In this chapter we are finishing up items for barrel installation and receiver support and alignment for the barrel. These are pretty much the final items that should complete the rifle. These installations are:

- Doing the Barrel Forcing Cone.

- Welding a lower panel onto the left receiver panel for the forward area beneath the barrel.

- Making a barrel bushing support for bracing of the chamber portion of the barrel to the front magazine guide.

- Welding a brace piece onto the barrel portion of each receiver panel.

- Making a front barrel clamp-lock setup for the forward end of the barrel.

- Attaching a side support rib to strengthen the receiver to barrel support.

- Do final welding of various tacked parts.

Barrel Forcing Cone

Now that the receiver is finished it is time to fit the barrel. Before we fit the barrel we should talk about the "Barrel Forcing Cone."

Back when I did "Homebuilt Firearms" I was concerned about small misalignments between the Bar Magazine chamber and the barrel. To compensate for that, I used a hand reamer to "funnel" or taper the entry hole in the barrel at the mouth of the Bar Magazine. My idea was to allow a slightly offset bullet to guide gradually into correct alignment for the path down the rest of the barrel. I figured this was a method to correct for my drilling of the bar magazine on a garage drill press.

It turns out this *exact same practice* is standard procedure for modern manufacture of revolver barrels to compensate for slight cylinder to barrel offsets, both in a new revolver and after wear. The Bar Magazine is basically a revolver cylinder in a straight line so the forcing cone concept seems entirely in line with present design practice!

If you look up "Revolver Barrel Forcing Cone " on the internet, many actual examples are given for all different firms and manufacturing methods, the angles vary, as well as the length of the coning. Essentially different manufacturers have different preferences. Basically, it comes down to such a span of acceptable methods that probably any variation of angle reaming or grinding is fine. Common tool angle values were 5, 11 and 18 degrees and in photos you can see the similarity to a common Hanson hand reamer as I used for the .22 design. In the Brownell cutter instructions, it recommends no more than .020 hole size over the size of a particular bullet..

That gives you a rough idea.

The Roto 4M barrel used for my carbine has a chamber cut into the breech. The diameter of the chamber is 0.476, whereas the bullet diameter (S.A.A.M. I.) is specified at 0.452 for a jacketed bullet. So, basically I felt a slight coning to adapt the chamber to the barrel at the front of the chamber area should be entirely reasonable. See Figure 57.

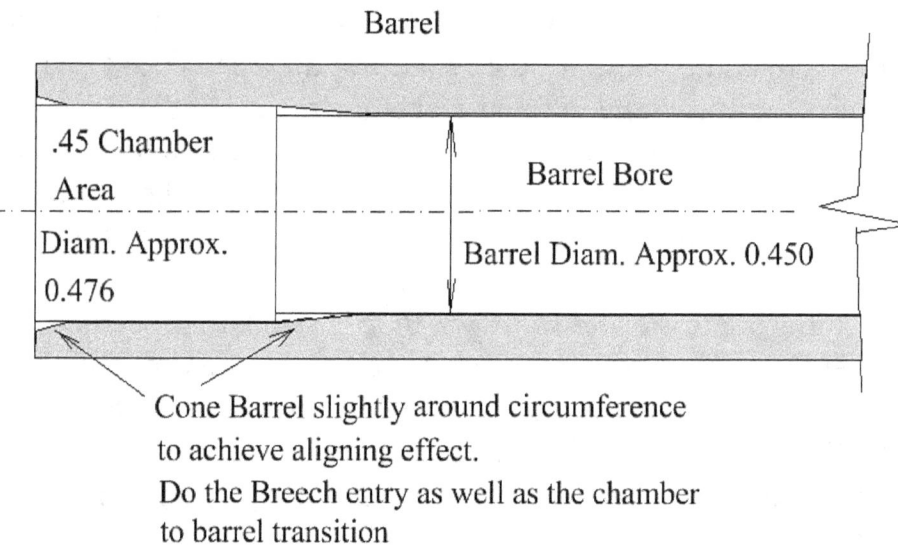

Cone Barrel slightly around circumference to achieve aligning effect.
Do the Breech entry as well as the chamber to barrel transition

Fig. 57. Roto 4M Barrel Forcing Cone.

****

Note: If using the other barrel from Green Mountain, the barrel forcing cone should be right at the beginning of the barrel, the breech end, just ahead of the Bar Magazine front guide.

****

Barrel Mounting

The Roto 4M barrel chamber end has a small nib that must be cut off with the angle grinder to allow a flat mate up with the receiver front guide hole. Do this carefully so the rear breech surface rests smoothly against the front magazine guide; do final fit with careful grinding or filing.

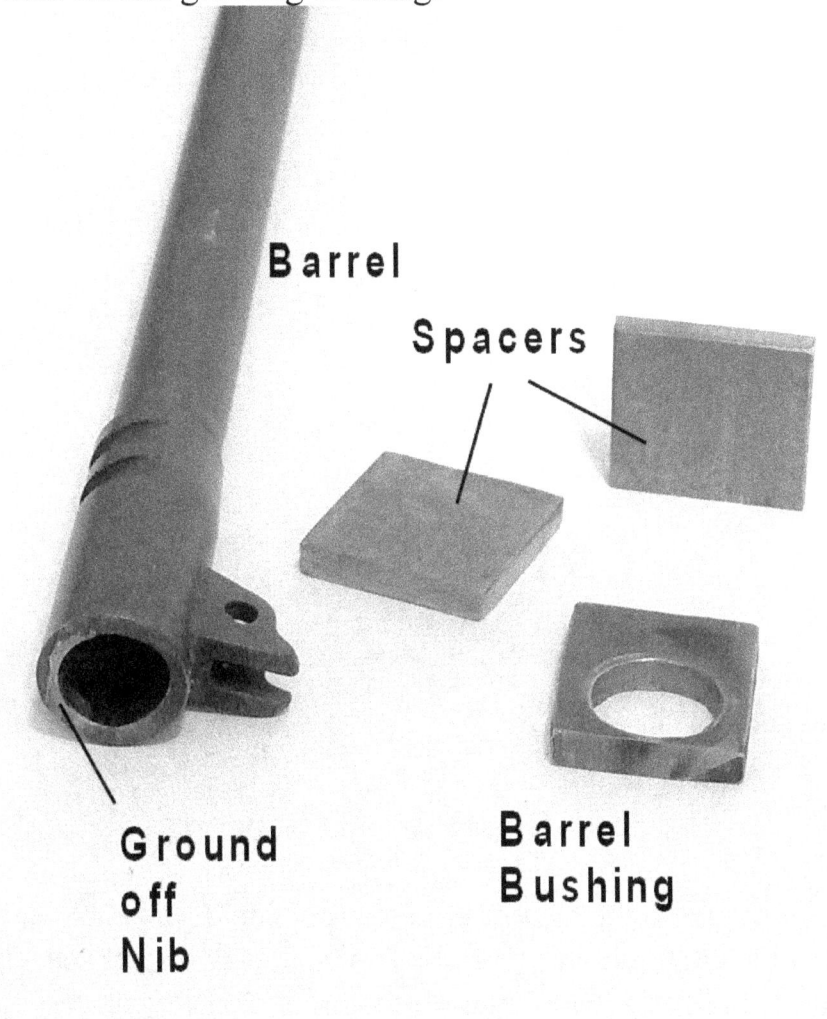

Fig. 58. Roto 4M Barrel and Barrel Support

In addition, with the Roto 4M barrel, you have a nice link fastening hole which can be pinned for a secure lock of the barrel to the receiver. However, this is of little use for secure pinning of the barrel against firing force. *I found that out during testing in Chapter 12, which led to the barrel bushing method described here.*

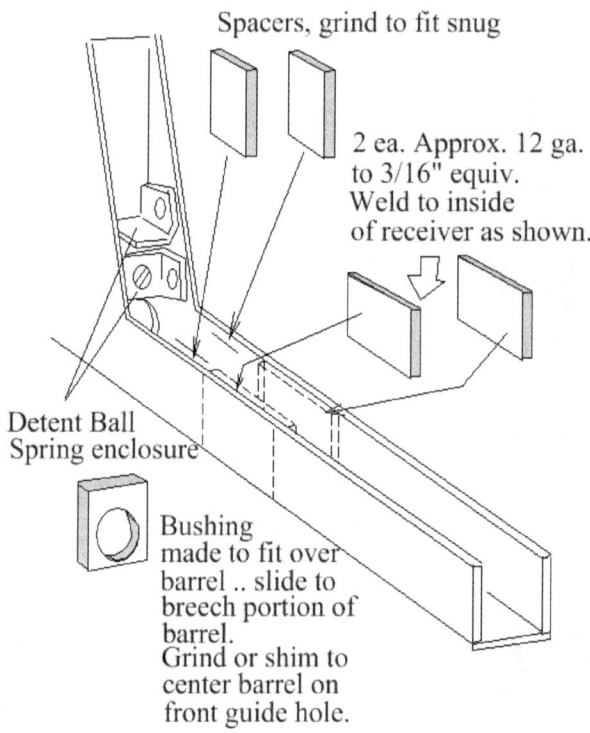

Fig. 59. Barrel Breech Support

See Figure 58, which shows the rear portion of the barrel and a barrel bushing made of 3/16" steel as well as two steel spacers.

(NOTE: If using the Green Mountain barrel, the barrel should be turned down by a Gunsmith or hobbyist friend with a lathe. In this case, leave a short portion at the breech of perhaps 0.9" diameter. You can then devise a locking means for secure attachment to the receiver.)

Next, Figure 59 shows where we are headed. Cut and tack weld a metal bottom strip perpendicular on the forward barrel portion of the left receiver to support and align the forward portion of the barrel , about 6 1/4" long. This will leave about a 2 inch open area underneath the breech portion of the receiver.

Next, make the 3/16" Steel barrel bushing support as shown in Figure 57 and 58. Drill it first to 1/2" and then enlarge using the stepless drill bit and file to fit and slide onto the barrel up to the breech. When carefully filed, the width and bottom can be file-set or shimmed to center the barrel to the front magazine guide hole. Braced as shown, with welded blocks on the forward portion of the receiver panels, and spacers to lock the barrel against the front guide, the barrel assembly will be entirely secure. A clamp will later hold the spacers securely in place.

Detailed Fit Up to the Receiver

I was concerned with good lineup of the barrel with the bar magazine. The approach here was to get a 7/16" metal or wood dowel rod (0.4377 Diameter...) to use inside the barrel for aligning it to the Bar Magazine chamber when in place, with the ball detent setting the alignment of the magazine. Then careful shimming with the spacer parts to eventually lock the barrel into good alignment should finalize the mounting setup. I wrapped some tape over the end that would fit into the Bar Magazine chamber to adjust to a snug fit there. The barrel fit was pretty good as is.

Adding masking tape to one end of the dowel insert until it fits snugly into the Bar Magazine chamber does work nicely. This is a simple method to facilitate aligning the barrel and allow the fabrication of the metal pieces and securing of the barrel.

Using your 7/16" dowel piece, wrap about 3/4" of the end with 4 or 5 turns of masking tape, then test the fit into your Bar

Magazine as you remove portions of the wrap. At some point, the tape end will slide into the chamber snugly, this is where you stop.

Place the Bar Magazine into the receiver. Push it down to lock the ball detent and align a chamber with the barrel hole. Next, slide the dowel into the barrel at the breech, untaped end first. As the taped end enters the breech a bit, stop.

Slide the barrel into place on the receiver assembly and then push the dowel rod so the taped end slides into the chamber in the Bar Magazine. It may require some grinding or shimming of the barrel bushing to true the barrel fit.... align and shim the barrel to the left receiver assembly, centered so the barrel is right against the front magazine guide and the dowel can slip in and out of the Bar Magazine. Assemble the other receiver panel and parts. Then grind or shim the spacer pieces to provide a good alignment.

Once the spacer shims are fitted, and a satisfactory alignment is achieved, remove the spacers and barrel assembly.

Make sure of placement of the two front brace pieces then clamp and weld onto the inside of the barrel shroud portion of the receiver panels. You can mount them a slight bit tighter to the spacer locations, and later grind the spacers for final fit.

These pieces will then form bracing for the later install of the spacers and barrel. Either grinding or shims can be used as needed to center the barrel correctly; do a good job.

Next we can do a lower bracket to pull the lower portion of the receiver panels together at the barrel breach.

Barrel Lock Brackets

See Figure 60 which gives a fairly good view with the other receiver panel.

It is now time to make the barrel breech side brackets... The Barrel Side Brackets in Figure 60 are about 3/4" x 1 3/4" in size, with a 1/8" drilled hole centered and about 3/8" from one end.

Assemble the right receiver panel over the barrel as it sits in place on the left receiver assembly. Mount a long 6-32 screw through the upper bracket, the barrel link hole and the lower bracket.

Cover the other surfaces carefully, preparing to clamp and tack weld the assembly.... once the barrel setup is confirmed they can be welded securely.

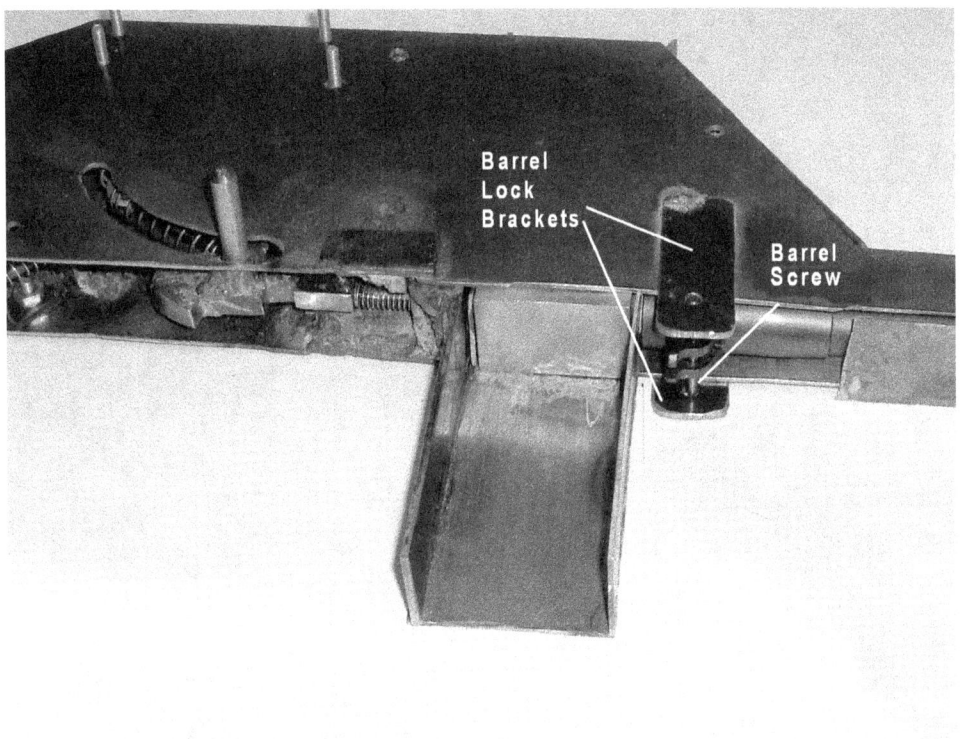

Fig. 60. Barrel Assembly Plan

Be careful that the barrel is fully seated as you align the two

brackets. At the forward end, make sure the barrel is set to level, and centered between the two receivers....

Fasten the barrel to hold the correct position on the front, with tape or some temporary means. Cover the barrel and area to protect the receiver panels. With the brackets in place, and the 6-32 screw through the holes, both sides, clamp and tack weld the receiver brackets in place temporarily.

Recheck the mounting, remove the barrel and finish welding the brackets.

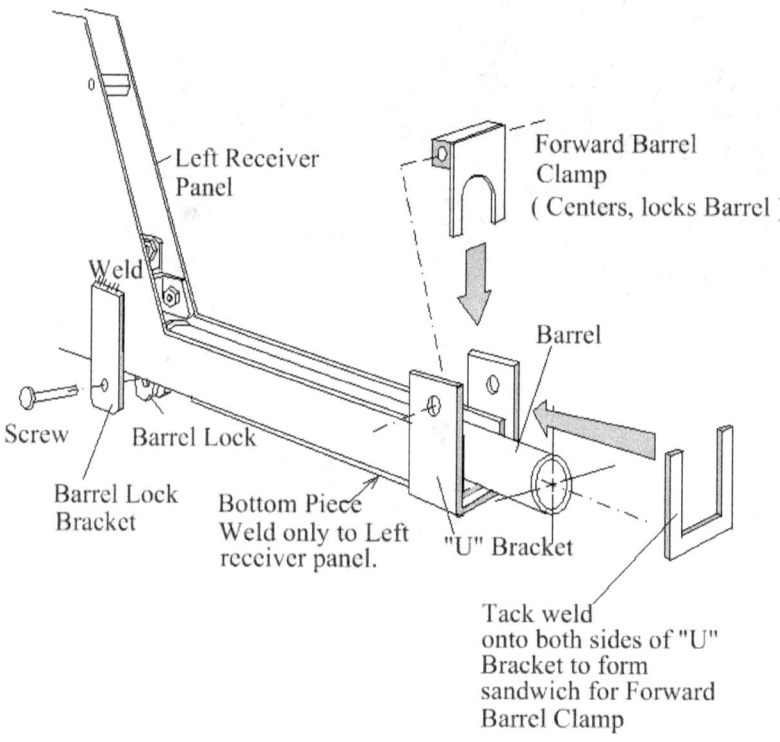

Fig. 61. Plan for Front Bracket

Front Barrel Bracket

Note the bottom flat portion covering the front bottom portion of the barrel... this is only welded to the one receiver panel, connection to the other panel can be done with some sort of bracket mounting. A front "U" bracket should now be made to center and lock the barrel securely at the front of the receiver.

This front bracket shown in Figure 61 will have a piece to snug the barrel ... it has to be carefully filed and fitted. Weld the clamp to the bottom barrel panel as shown. If you weld the front "U" barrel clamp slightly forward of the ends of the receiver panels leaving an area for the Forward Barrel Clamp to slide down between, you can rig a very solid forward clamp as shown in Figures 61. You will be able to slide it down into the "U" clamp and by welding a bit of cap over the front of the "U" clamp, the forward clamp-lock will be sandwiched in with only one cross screw.

Fig. 62. Front Barrel clamping

At this point, you will note the receiver and barrel are not rigid enough. What is needed is a perfectly straight "strongback" rib running lengthwise down the side from the rear portion of the receiver to the front portion alongside the barrel. This will stiffen the rifle considerably using only a 1/2" wide rib welded along the left side. It should be welded horizontally so it sticks out perpendicular to the left receiver panel. See Figure 63 for the general idea. Weld for a half inch then let it cool... space about 2 inches and do another... let it cool... this avoids welding all hot and as the metal cools it contracts and curves the barrel support.

Be sure to grind the piece true for straightness and also place a slight notch for the barrel brace, and any weld blemishes that are raised.

A shorter version of a stiffening rib should be welded onto the right receiver panel as well. This will further strengthen the barrel to receiver portion of the carbine and also provide mounting for securing the barrel spacers later.

Round off the front and rear outer edge and smooth so no burrs are present. Check the barrel fit, anything else on the assembly, finish welding any tacked on parts securely. Grind any rough edges and carefully remove any debris, beads, to get to a satisfactory point; file any melt through bumps that might impede any mechanism.

Weld on a piece to cover the left side of the lower magazine guides, (left receiver panel...) being sure of clearance for the Bar Magazine. See Figure 63. This is one weld locking the rear guide in place.

Also weld a piece to cover the lower magazine guides that will be part of the right receiver panel. Other pieces to cover openings here and there, etc. will be done after test firing the rifle!

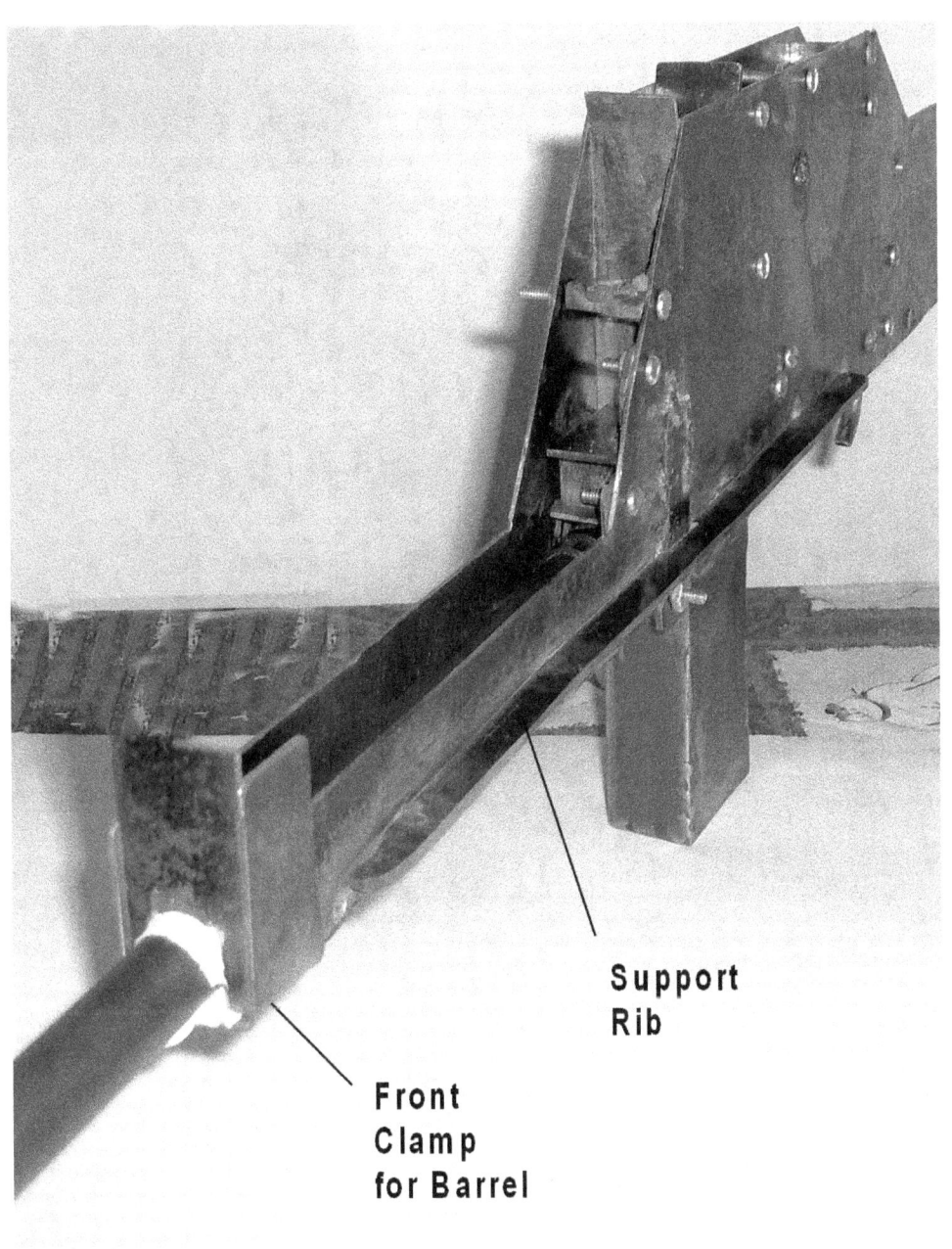

Fig. 63. Barrel Support Rib (Strongback..)

Fig. 64. Right Magazine Cover

Chapter 11

On Using the Springs

Now is a good time to discuss the springs. When I did the .22 version of this rifle, the situation was trickier. I had made a narrow receiver setup to accommodate a 1/2" thick Bar Magazine. With this narrow a space, the hammer assembly and several items rubbed a bit, there were friction points, even the springs rubbed the receiver panels. It was very tricky to establish good free motion.

I had examined revolvers I own and estimated the "feel" of cocking a hammer as at most perhaps 5 lbs pull, in a rotation arc of about 1 1/2 " or so. Springs come with ratings, such as 5 lbs per inch, that sort of thing... the "Spring Specification." As long as the spring is not overstressed, that is its value for the amount of compression or tension.

This was how I bought the springs from Amazon.com, from the Industrial/ Scientific section, or other suppliers; even ranch and hardware stores sometimes have bins of hardware including springs. They come in many lengths and strengths. This design requires compression springs.

With my view towards the swinging "T" arm and hammer, I settled on several experimental springs when I did the .22 rifle.

Now, with the .45 version, I had that previous bunch of springs plus a better feel for what I needed. My feeling is to go with springs in about the 5 to 10 lb per inch category, this pretty much dictates .038 to .048 thickness wire springs, either Music Wire or Stainless Steel. Lengths needed are about 3 inches and 1 inch for these... for the hammer spring and the ball detent, respectively.

- For the ball detent, a 1/2" diameter x 1" long is ideal.

- The 3" long sizes are fine for the "T" hammer assembly and need to develop pretty good force over the arc of about 2 1/2" .

- As to diameters... 0.3" diameter would be a minimum or 3/8" to 1/2" diameter ideal for the hammer spring. My second setup used nested springs, a 0.3"D x 2 1/2"L x 0.042 wire and a 7/16"D x 3"L x 0.048 wire spring.

The .45 version has a huge advantage over the .22 version, too, in lack of side friction areas on the receiver... mostly all hammer and other actions are in air between the 0.9" gap between the panels! The only hammer friction then is the pivot point. It is fairly minimal not being out on the lever arm. Friction of the Positioner is minimal compared to the force to push down a cartridge against the ball detent and side friction of the Bar Magazine.

The other springs can be of small strength... the Ace Hardware assortment 5213517 is ideal for the remainder of springs.

The assortment has a couple fairly small springs that are strong... one of these is ideal for the hammer release mechanism spring. Some small little springs are ideal for the Positioner spring, and for the small spring on the top of the "T" Bar.

There is a 1/2" small spring which worked as a demo for the detent ball, but is insufficient in strength.

However there are ways to add to spring strength:

- Nestle one or more smaller springs *within* a larger spring, or
- Add springs in series if distance is allowable, perhaps with a washer between.
- Or combinations of these two.

Also in some cases you can apply a ***pre-compression***, where the springs remain partially compressed before the mechanism moves. (Use a longer spring than the initial space before movement ...)

We have *only two* truly critical springs in this carbine; the ball detent spring and the hammer spring.

Ball Detent Spring

In the case of the ball detent spring, I used nestled springs of different diameters. That combined with the chamber lock device will insure a reliable locking alignment of the cartridge with the barrel. The outside spring is the dark colored weak 1/2" diameter one about 1" long that comes with the Ace Assortment, one inner spring is a longer, stiffer, approximately 1 1/4" spring from that same assortment, about 0.375" in diameter, and a third is also from the assortment, in between those two diameters... up to three springs that nestle and add force to the ball detent! See Figure 65 on the next page.

The space inside for the ball detent is about 1 inch, but keep in mind the ball itself takes up a part of that space. That means the springs involved are already compressed even before the Bar Magazine moves out of lock position. This gives a fairly strong lock of the mechanism, however for an absolute correct keying of a chamber spot, the chamber lock mechanism is still absolutely necessary. A single spring could also work fine for the ball detent, probably in 0.038 or 0.042 wire.

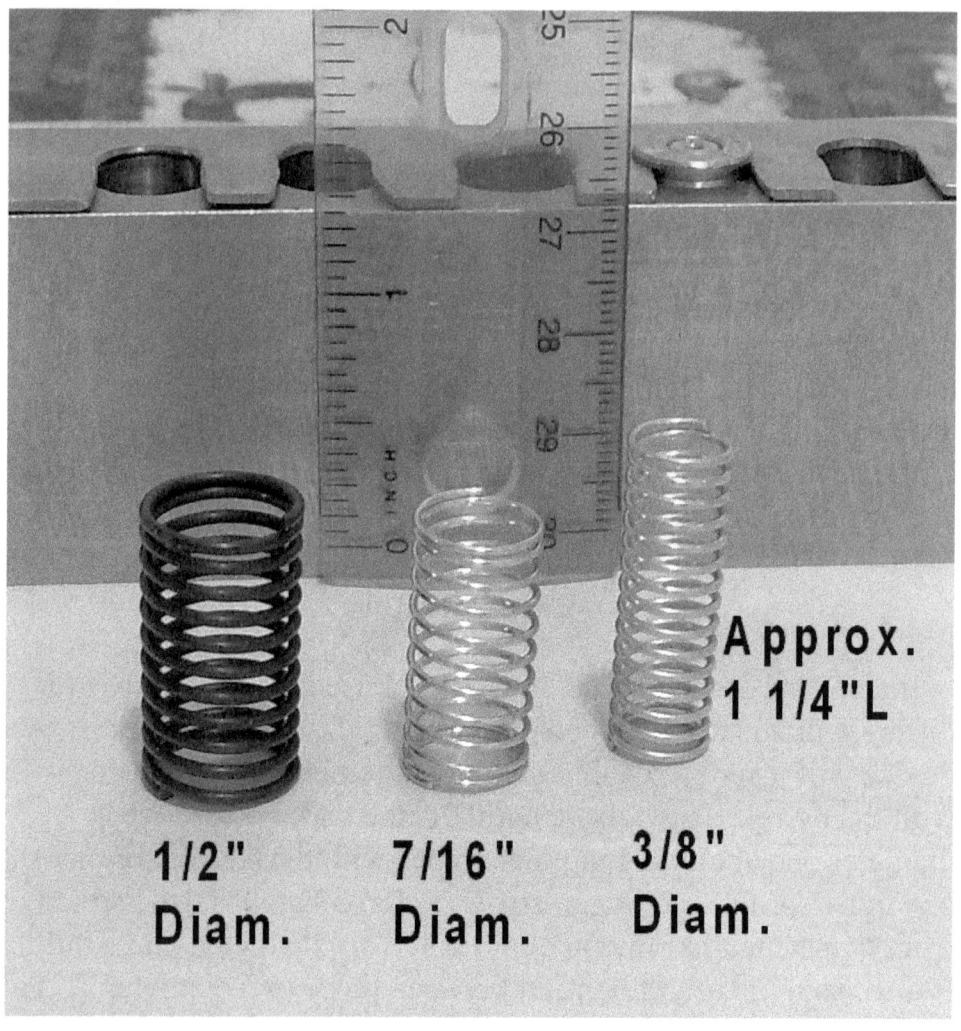

Fig. 65. Possible Springs For Ball Detent

The Hammer Spring

The hammer spring must be capable of driving the hammer to fire a round, it has a good arc of swing so the situation is ideally suited for a long spring setup. There is a guide rod, so this does add some additional consideration. I had purchased two springs from Amazon.com initially in the 1 1/2" length. With the long arc the "T" bar swings, I thought two springs with a washer between should be about right. However, after problems in testing, I revised the design. Look at Figure 66, which shows the longer spring setup I next used for the hammer.

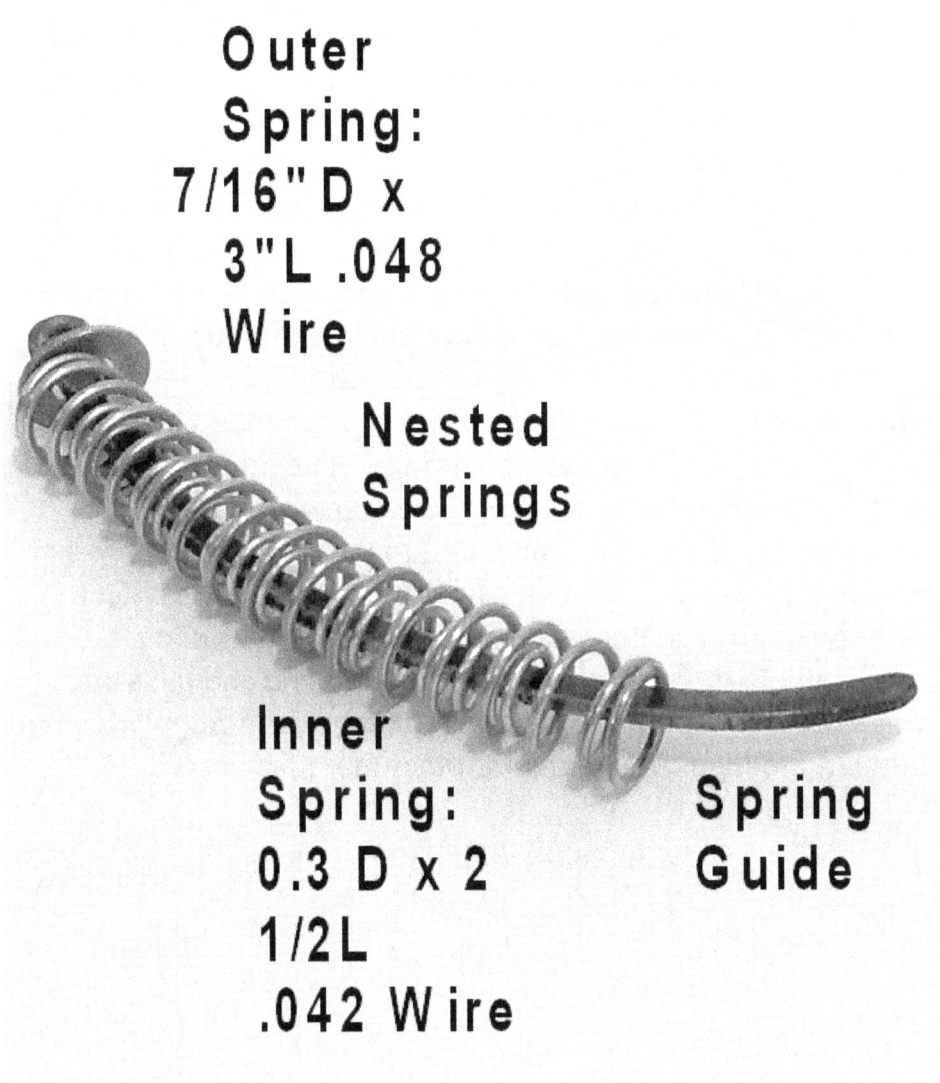

Fig. 66. Spring For Hammer

The springs shown were obtained from the hardware bins at a local hardware store; (Wilco...) they are Hillman 540012 and 540114 parts.

There are springs larger than .048 wire also, and perhaps one of these would work in place of the two hammer springs I used in this phase. If too strong, you can permit a gap to allow some movement before spring compression begins. (You cannot use pre-compression in the hammer spring as it will push the firing pin into the magazine area, causing an obstruction.)

I intend to experiment further during future testing with various options. You can see there are many choices here. I got a Hillman #540533 spring in 0.054 wire that may work nicely.

If one spring works in place of the two I used, it would offer less rubbing between springs. Every change provides a chance to improve operation, simplicity or reliability.

Similar units are available from Amazon, in the Industrial and Scientific Section, Compression Springs. The important thing is length and diameter of wire... for the hammer assembly essentially 3 inch lengths, and 0.042 to 0.048 or larger wire size. They are typically available in Music Wire or Stainless Steel.

Amazon shows compression springs from Small Parts Inc. and Reid Supply (ReidSupply.com) amongst others, and the same springs I found in bins at a Wilco Hardware/Farm Supply (Hillman) are likely standards for other manufacturers as well.

Chapter 12

Testing the Rifle Mechanism..
and Correcting problems

Once the entire receiver is finished and the barrel is added, it is time to test the rifle! The basic approach here will be to temporarily mount the rifle setup onto a wooden base so it can be fired from a distance with a pull string. The base will be weighted or secured so it will be stable.

Now we can install the hammer spring... all those photos showing a spring in place were only for the purpose of illustration, because **once those springs are installed, the rifle can shoot and is DANGEROUS!**

Figure 66 shows a basic approach to the base assembly made from some scrap wood. It should hold the rifle from tipping sideways and also have a rear support to absorb any recoil. The height of the two vertical supports is designed to keep the rifle fairly vertical front to rear, with a notched slot for the barrel and receiver portions. With these guides custom fitted, the rifle can rest on its protruding magazine enclosure and the two vertical supports will hold it quite well.

I rounded up a roll of strong cord string, and recommend at least 50 feet, or perhaps 100 feet.

You must locate a safe area out in the country or a place you can shoot it with no danger to any property or anyone. I am lucky living in the West, Oregon in fact, where there are many secluded wooded National Forest areas that are located far from any people or any safety hazardous areas.

Once you secure such a location, find a dirt bank or large stump, something of large mass and thickness as a backstop for the rounds to bury themselves into... penetration of a .45 round could be many inches; you want to to be very safe and have plenty of back berm.

Set up the test base and mount your rifle mechanism so it will aim into the berm or backstop. Place a rock or some weight onto the front and rear of the test base to hold it down.

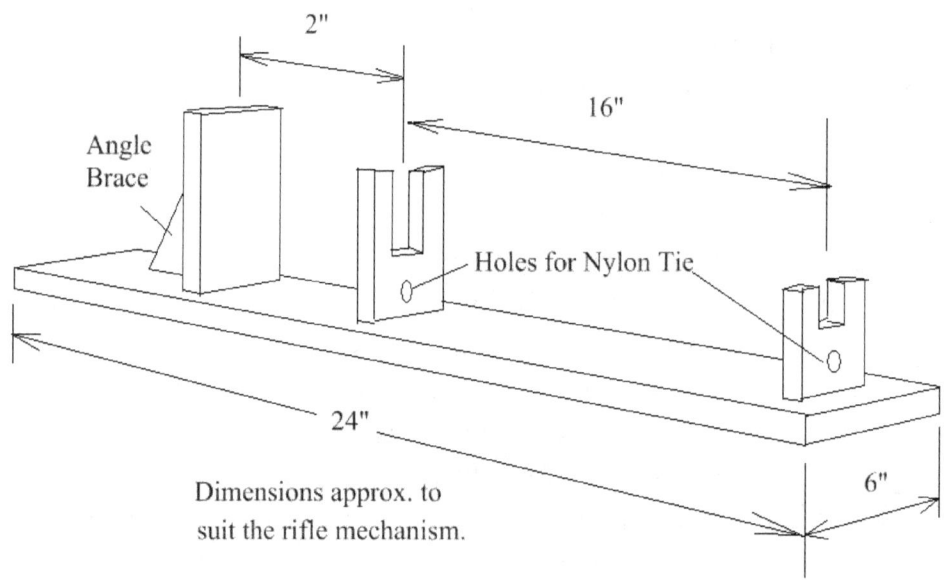

Fig. 67. Typical Base Jig to Hold Rifle

Connect one end of your pull string to the trigger, tape it a bit to be sure it will stay secured. Walk back unwinding string to your safe firing location, and lay the other end there for your test.

Load your Bar Magazine with rounds, using the rim lock clip for securing of the rounds. Take a last look at your rifle setup and be sure it is safely secure with the rifle barrel facing the dirt berm. Load your magazine into the rifle, being careful the rear of the cartridges are facing back with the end gap at the top where the indexing hole lies in front. Slowly push the magazine down until the ball detent grabs the first hole. You are ready.

Grasp the receiver and pull the cocking handle back with your right hand to cock the rifle... you should feel the clunk of the magazine as it sets into place for the first round, and hear a secure click as the hammer release grabs the hammer. Slowly let off on the cocking lever to be sure it has grabbed, and then head back to your safe spot for pulling the string. (Don't tangle in the string on your way back...)

This is it....

Pull the string....!! That first round should fire! If the rifle setup jumps, anchor it a bit better. Go check for anything unusual in the setup, does the barrel appear fine, no apparent damage anywhere.... If so, repeat the cock for another shot.

Continue the test for the remaining four rounds, checking after each test firing, then operate the cocking lever part way to release the magazine from the rifle. After releasing the magazine, be sure the hammer is released. Also check for loosened screws after a few shots, you may decide later to weld certain brackets that are mounted with screws if they loosen... or use Locktite. If the part or bracket needs to be removable for repairs ever, use the Locktite.

Examine the Bar Magazine and barrel carefully for anything unusual. If everything looks fine, it is probably a good idea to do several more firings, with inspection checks at each shot and an additional examination of the bar and barrel after each five shots.

At some point, a confidence will take over, you will be wanting to finish your rifle. It is time to build and install the stock.

But first, a discussion of problem areas.

Problems Observed

Note: These are problems I encountered!

- Hammer Springs Initially I had too weak a hammer spring setup in the rifle; these were two 2" series springs of 0.038 wire, and when looking at the dimples in the rounds, it was apparent the strikes were too light. With using two 2" springs with a washer between... the washer also caused extra friction. I went to .042 wire... still not adequate with even lighter springs nested inside. The fix: ***nested 3"L 0.048 wire spring, 7/16" diameter approx. ...and an inner 0.3" D x 2 1/2"L spring of 0.042 wire. This gave good impact, solid firing, no middle washer friction. Keep in mind you may experiment further for a suitable fix. (Single spring perhaps... as discussed in Chapter 11.)***

- Barrel Shifting With only one firing in my test, I found my barrel had shifted forward, actually bending the cross pin securing it to the two receiver brackets! Even a hardened pin bent due to bullet friction moving forward in the barrel! This makes you realize the force you are dealing with is huge, and not to be ignored! The pin is not enough lock for the front edge of the Roto 4M enlarged barrel area at the breech. I revised the build in Chapter 10 to eliminate the problem. The fix: ***I ended up drilling a 3/16" thick steel piece with*** *a 1/2" diameter bit then filing and grinding with a Dremel Tool to make a barrel collar, a full round bushing (filing required to fit..) for the barrel just forward of the breech. This piece could then be slid over the barrel and mounted with support and solidly braced by welded pieces and spacers on each receiver panel, which allowed a secure correction.*

- Ball Detent   I noted on a few occasions the detent ball came out and was kiddie-cornered by the springs in its compartment ... this required a method of locking the spring alignment to the ball axis... The fix: *either restricting side play area between the two receiver panels, or providing a guide for the spring. See Figure 68, for one solution. I actually used side spacers in mine.*

- Firing Pin   My original version had a pin epoxied into the side as a stop instead of the one piece stepped type shown back in Figure 31. It came out, allowing the firing pin to jam the operation. The fix: *I ended up welding a small nib onto it making it the equivalent of Figure 31, chapter 6.*

- Front Magazine Guide   I originally had a thin front guide... It bulged slightly inward due to the heavy pressure of firing, and began binding the Bar Magazine. The fix: *I cut the original front guide out and replaced it with a heavier steel piece, about*
- *0.010 inches thick... 12 gauge. This necessitated re-drilling the two holes as described in chapter 4. Chapter 4 was corrected to show the thicker front guide.*

- Bullet Jacket Shavings The various flaws above on a few occasions caused misalignment and some shearing of bullet jackets. This did not appear to cause any damage to the barrel or front guide, but did jam the Bar magazine. I believe correcting the other items will essentially correct this.

- Loosening Screws Also check for loosened screws after a few shots. The fix: ***To weld certain brackets that are mounted with screws if they loosen... or use Locktite on the screws. If the part or bracket needs to be removable for repairs ever, use the Locktite. But brackets or pieces that should never need replacement can be welded, such as the upper bracket in Figure 68.***

- Lower Hammer Arm The lower hammer arm was bending during cocking; the fix: ***Welding a reinforcing rib along the front portion of the lower arm. See Figure 69.***

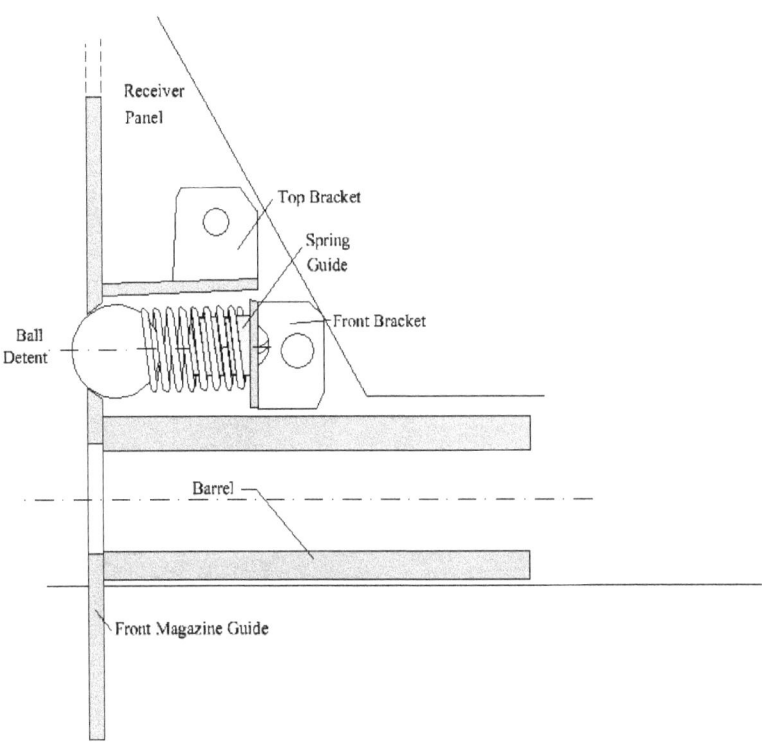

Fig. 68. Ball Detent Guide

Fig. 69. Reinforced Hammer

Chapter 13

Building the Stock
With pistol grip

With the barrel mounted and functioning, it is time to do some finishing ... the stock comes now. Look at Figure 70 , which shows the grid sketch plan for building a one piece stock with pistol grip.

The stock I built is laminated of two pieces of 1/2" plywood with strips of 1/4" Ash laminated over both sides. It ended up being approximately 1 7/16" thick after shaping. Of course you have any option here depending on your preferences... you may like a thicker stock or whatever you wish.

Once you have cut out the material with a Jigsaw or Sabre Saw, apply wood glue and clamp the inner core pieces securely together for a couple hours.

Next apply your desired outer layers, once again clamping the layers together to allow the glue to cure.

Once dry, set the stock over your receiver piece to decide where you can thin it in the receiver area to assemble the rifle. Align the pistol grip so it is in the correct geometry for applying trigger pull. Mark your area where the wood is too thick. You will need to rout or remove those areas to allow clearance.

While your laminated assembly is flat, it is easier to cut some of the excess thickness off the front. Remember, the receiver is about 0.9" wide in between panels, so you must thin the front

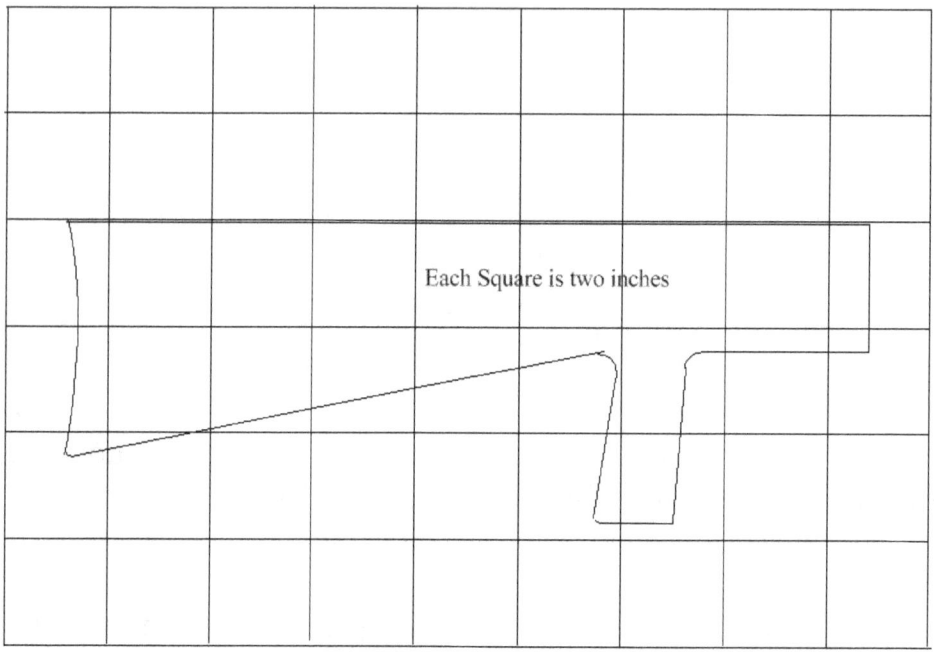

Fig. 70. Scaled Plan for Pistol Grip Stock

portion of the stock, and also make room for some of the inner mechanisms, especially the trigger and hammer release. If you set the blade on a table saw to allow removing a bit from each side, you can run the front section through allowing close kerf cuts that can be removed with in-between continued cuts or chiseling.

You likely will not be able to remove every bit you need to take off, particularly around the pistol grip. Here you may need to rout the excess away or use some chisel removal. Use clamped on pieces to limit your cutting area as necessary, you do not wish to damage anything beyond the area inside the receiver panels. When the area appears satisfactory on thickness, it is time to remove any areas that would interfere with the operating parts. In my case a router was used here too. You can shorten your rear portion of the receiver panels at this point to allow a mounting setup consistent with the pistol grip and trigger placement. In my case I needed to drill a hole for the no. 1 spacer... you will need to determine these sorts of things based on your finished piece. Slight differences in construction will force different solutions, but you get the idea.

You can sand and finish the stock with your favorite finish.

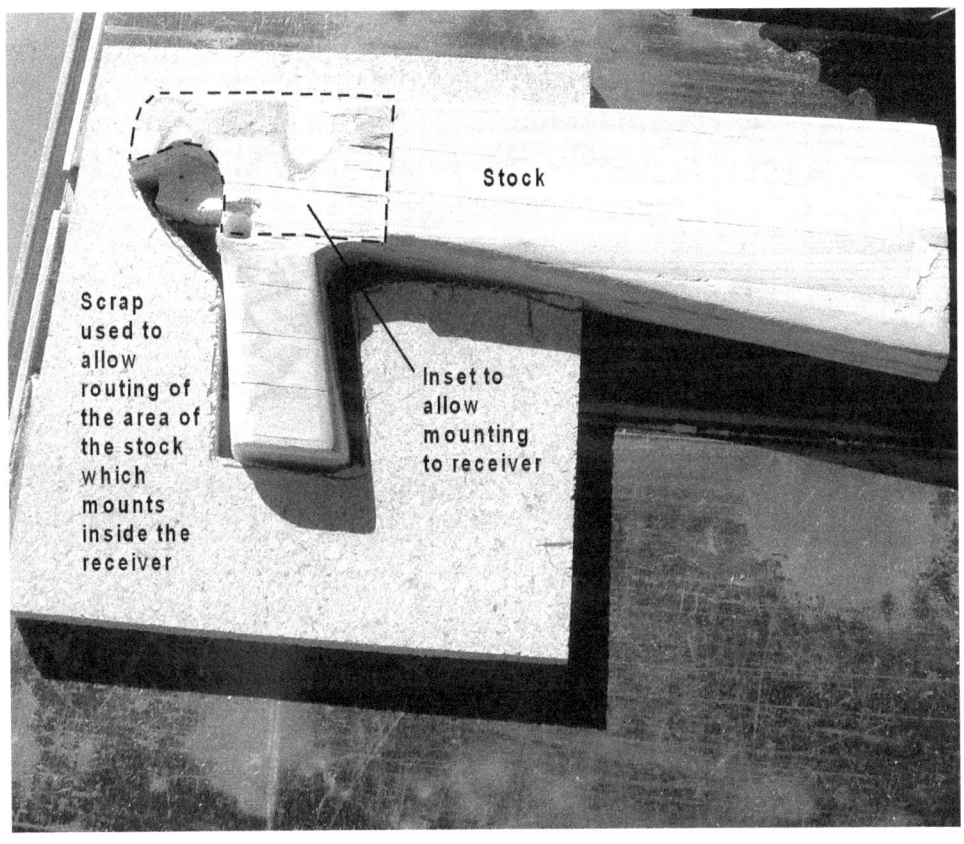

Fig. 71. Partially Routed Stock

Look at Figure 71 to see how mine ended up. I routed out a portion to clear the hammer release and the trigger, (I also removed a portion of the Steel trigger which was originally built for my rifle version in "Homebuilt Firearms.")

In some cases you run into some interference; a spacer has a fillet of welding at the bottom holding it to the receiver so you must cut out a bit at that area of the wood surface... beyond your drilled hole... that sort of thing.

Once you have solved these small fit-up problems and get the stock mounted, you may either do only a barrel clamp and protective plate below the barrel-to-front-guide interface... or you could also do a foregrip for the barrel portion ahead of the receiver. Look at Figure 72 . Sand and round corners if you do this piece.

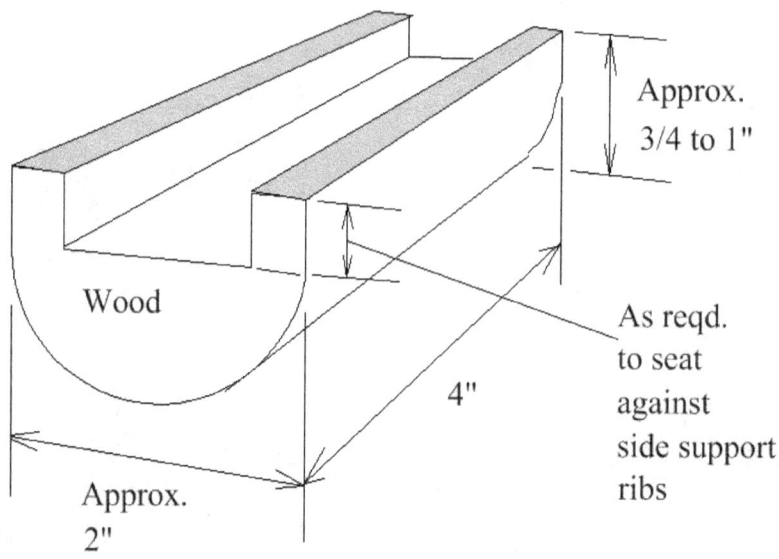

Slot width to match
lower portion of receiver
barrel shroud

Fig. 72. Typical Foregrip

Chapter 14

Finishing Up

There are only a few items to finish now, I believe:

- A lower protective plate at the barrel junction,

- Sights, and a rear receiver cover...

- A trigger guard,

- A carrying handle,

- A clamp ring to lock the barrel spacers,

- A few covers over the receiver where desired.

Protective Plate

I welded a protective 14 gauge panel onto the front portion of the lower magazine guide pieces that are welded onto the front and rear magazine guides. The purpose is to protect the shooter in case of a fragment or debris flying out from beneath the barrel breech. It is a shield just in case. Revolvers sometimes spit out fragments where the cylinder meets the barrel. Leave no holes, use Epoxy or filler if needed.. See Figure 73.

I also welded a piece at the top rear of the left receiver to block any debris from coming out the rear in case a spring broke or any other failure; at the top is a peep sight hole to form the rear sight as well. See Figure 74.

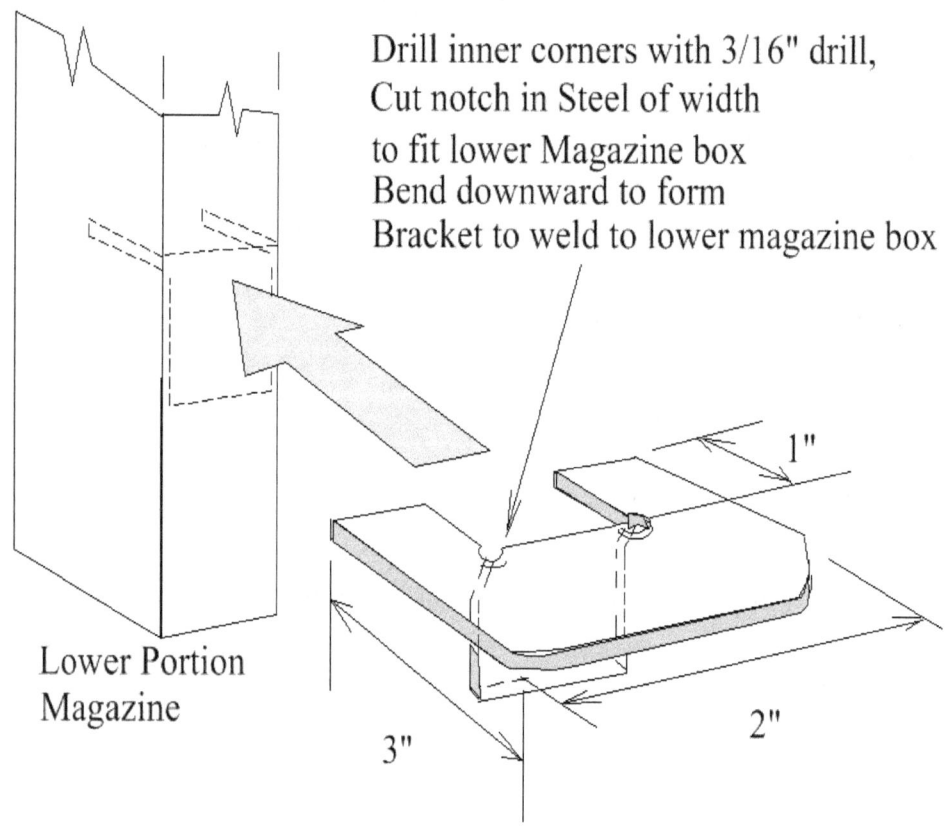

Fig. 73. Protective Plate Below Breech

Fig. 74. Rear Peep Sight and Receiver Cover

Trigger Guard

The trigger guard I added to my receiver was attached as in Figure 75 to the rear bottom screw of the Bar Magazine lock pin bracket, and the stock handgrip. It is nothing more than a strip bent to allow trigger movement while enclosing the finger inside.

A strip of 14 gauge steel about 4 1/2"L x 1/2" W is used, bent to allow joining and protecting the trigger area. Any method works as long as it doesn't interfere with movement of parts, etc.

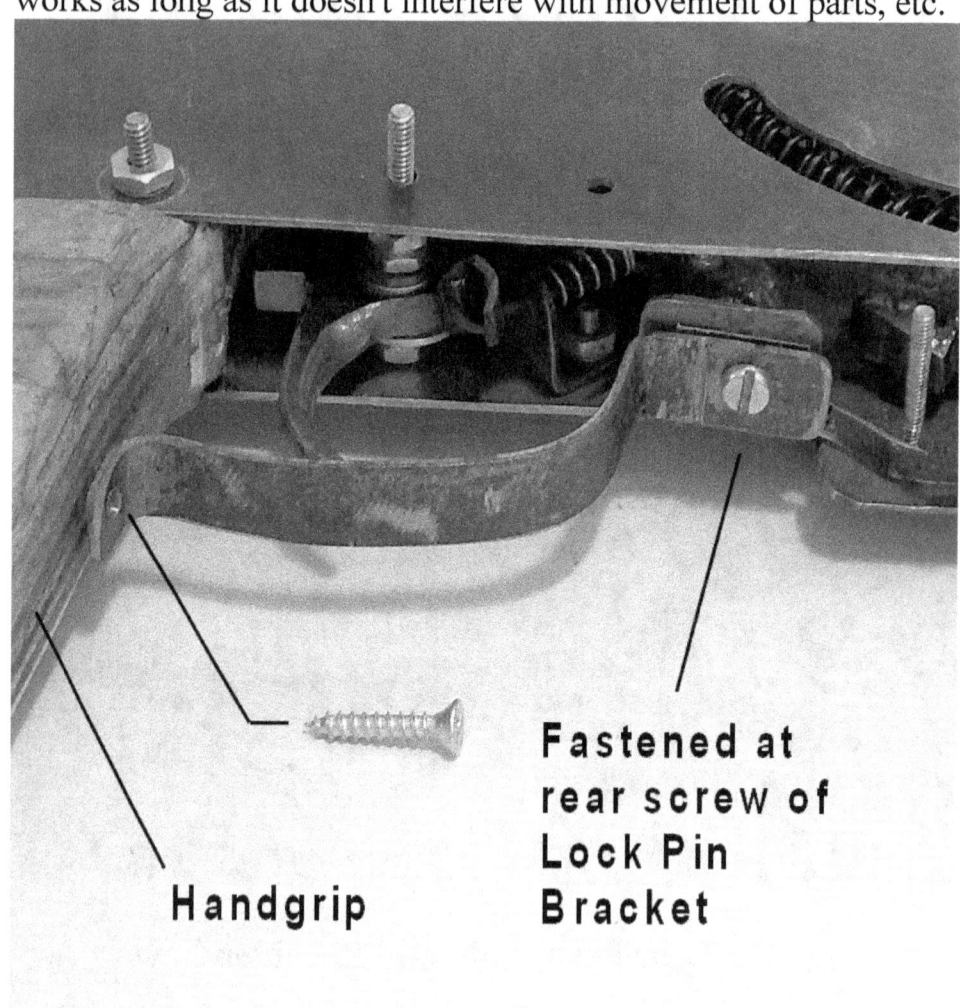

Fig. 75. Typical Trigger Guard Mounting

Carrying Handle

A carrying handle can be added to the left side of the receiver basically in the front half... it should be mounted at a fairly balanced point for your build. The carrying handle pieces that

Fig. 76. Carrying Handle

are welded onto the left receiver panel in my assembly are about

5/8"W x about 3/4"L of 12 gauge steel. They are rounded at the outside edge and drilled for #10 screws prior to welding them on.

The wooden handle is a large dowel, about 4 3/4" L x 1" Diameter. If you drill a 7/16" hole lengthwise and cut a long strip of 12 gauge that will fit through, you can bend it and slide it through one end, bend the other and make a similar handle to that shown in Figure 76.

Upper Clamp for Barrel Spacers

The spacers which lock the barrel into place with the barrel bushing must be secured so they won't fall out. This takes a simple top clamp to secure the pieces; this device is shown in Figure 77, and mounts through the side stiffeners on the receiver panels. It takes some care in bending but by this time we are used to making and bending small parts like this one.
These would be ideal screws to use Locktite with for securing the nuts and lock washers.

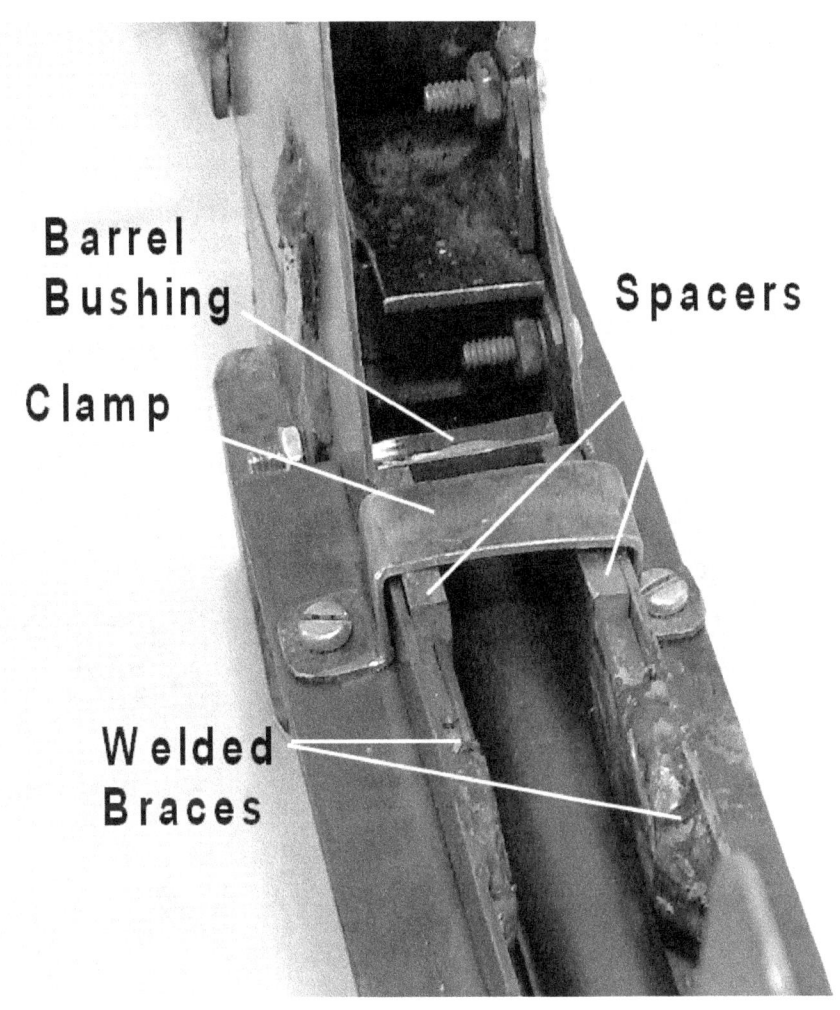

Fig. 77. Clamp for Barrel Spacers

A Front Sight

The final significant item is the front sight, which can be attached to the front barrel clamp fixture. A simple windage adjustment can be made for the front or rear sight by threading the movable portion of the sight so turning a screw moves it right and left. See Figure 78 . The side supports are not threaded.

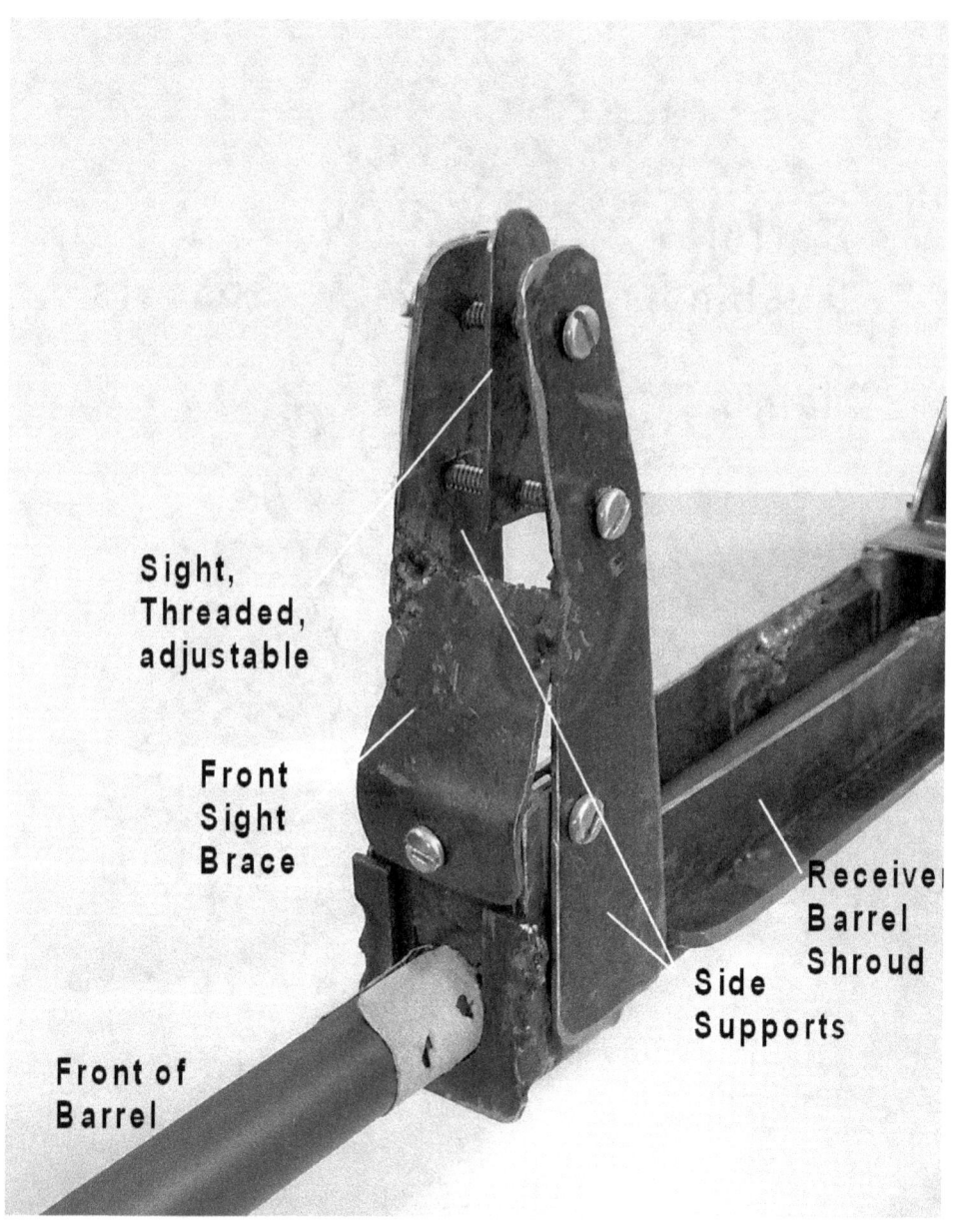

Fig. 78. A Possible Front Sight

Installing nuts on the outside with thread lock makes for an adjustable sight. A welded portion attaches to the side supports and fastens to the front of the forward barrel clamp. This makes it fairly secure. The elevation of the sight can be filed to setup for the typical range.

Remaining Covers to Protect Mechanisms

There is an exposed area at the bottom of the rifle where the magazine lock pin springs are... this could be covered so your hands will not block the lock function.
I did not cover mine as I wished it to be open to display the inner workings when showing it at gun shows, so this is a judgment call for each builder.

Final comments

This pretty much finishes the construction. At this point, it is good to go over the rifle and smooth rough welds, and corners perhaps, I certainly know my welds are not too attractive. A person could touch up here and there with a little bluing.
I did not do a front forepiece ahead of the magazine area, it felt comfortable holding the magazine guide with the forward hand. It also saved some weight not having a forepiece. The rifle is fairly light actually, as I used thin sheet for the receiver panels, possibly lighter than 14 gauge.
This rifle is not perfect; instead it is a beginning experiment in building and fabrication with the idea towards showing the use of garage tools in producing a working rifle in a significant caliber.
It is not a gun with an expected lifetime of thousands of rounds. It is not something you would use to go hunting Grizzly bears in Alaska, that would only be after very careful testing in cold weather, with this being a last ditch survival weapon. There are so many things ... spring strength in the cold, little problems that I ran into during testing, screws loosening, etc.

It is definitely a good idea to weld all brackets and mechanism pieces inside if they are unlikely to need repair. I welded the upper bracket for the hammer release, the upper enclosure for the detent ball spring, anything that is mounted and likely to not have significant wear... after all, this will not be a primary firearm, it is just fun to build and learn about the technique as we find we can make a real firearm.

Many screws that are mounted through the left receiver panel can also be tack welded for stability. The nuts and lock washers are not sufficient without Locktite for parts you might wish to remove possibly, so be sure to use thread lock on those.

Final views of my rifle are shown in Figures 79 through 80. The rifle is 37" long, the metal receiver is 4" high. I still must grind off excess screw lengths, etc. and do some final finishing.

During the building and typical use of the rifle a person will perhaps get ideas of better, simpler parts and designs, some improvements... *that is the whole purpose of a project like this...* it is a fabulous, fun building and learning experience. It is to show it can be done.

As a person fires it and gains confidence, perhaps making improvements along the way, they will find it functions pretty well, and is indeed a occasional use experimental rifle in a considerable, hefty caliber!

When shooting the rifle the shooter should always wear safety glasses and use ear protection... standard practice in shooting! The usual rules of safe shooting apply.

Have fun and be safe!